Disciples Together

Disciples Together

Discipleship, Formation and
Small Groups

Roger L. Walton

scm press

Published in 2014 by SCM Press
Editorial office
3rd Floor
Invicta House
108–114 Golden Lane
London
EC1Y 0TG

SCM Press is an imprint of Hymns Ancient & Modern Ltd
(a registered charity)
13A Hellesdon Park Road
Norwich NR6 5DR

www.scmpress.co.uk

British Library Cataloguing in Publication data

A catalogue record for this book is available
from the British Library

978 0 334 05182 4

Typeset by Regent Typesetting
Printed and bound by
CPI Group (UK) Ltd, Croydon

Dedicated to my wife Marion,
my friend and spiritual companion of over 40 years

Contents

Introduction   ix

Section 1: Formation   1

1   Forming Christian Disciples: Mission   3
2   Forming Christian Disciples: Worship   16
3   Forming Christian Disciples: Community   28
4   Forming Christian Disciples: Christian Education   41
Reflections and Questions on Section 1   62

Section 2: Small Groups and Discipleship Formation   67

5   The Value of Small Groups   69
6   Small Group Explosion: Church Small Groups in
    the Twentieth Century   85
7   Research on Church-related Small Groups   108
8   Small Groups and Discipleship Formation   123

9   Disciples Together: Small Groups in Theological
    Perspective   138

Bibliography   157

Introduction

Go down to the potter's house, and there I will let you hear my words.

Jeremiah 18.2

The first church I served as a minister was in Stourbridge. This is an area of the West Midlands famous for its cut glass. When I moved on to my next appointment, several kind people gave me pieces of cut glass – bowls, wine glasses and ornaments – made at one of the many glassworks in the area. I still have them some 40 years later. Sometimes I lift them from the shelves they adorn and hold them, feeling the weight of the glass and the smooth and etched surfaces of these works of art. I continue to be captivated by their elegance and fine craftsmanship and see in my mind's eye the skilled worker who created the shapes and patterns they carry. I reimagine the visits I paid to glass-blowing demonstrations and the sense of wonder I felt watching these experts handle molten glass, turning, blowing, reheating, cooling and fashioning, at ease with their skill – and making it look easy – as they created objects of beauty before my eyes. I could watch such craft in action for hours.

Had glass-blowing been a part of the economy of Jeremiah's home town in the sixth century BCE, I wonder if God might have prompted him to visit the glass-blower's workshop rather than the potter's house. The point of the visit would have been the same, no doubt. For what Jeremiah saw – a potter making a pot that went wrong and was refashioned into another object – reminded him that God was forming Israel and that he would shape his people according to his purpose. Jeremiah would have witnessed similar creative and redemptive acts in the glass-blower's workshop. But he also would have seen that there is more in this forming process than the material and the hands of the craftsman. Perhaps he would have reflected on the roles of fire, breath and water – all symbols of the work of the Spirit – in the creative process. Maybe he would have noticed the various tools brought into play at different stages to work with these natural elements. Although not complex in the modern scientific sense of the word, he would possibly have observed and commented on the range of skills and processes the craftsperson must skilfully apply at the right time. He might, like me, have felt quiet awe observing the worker's ability to combine and use the various elements, energies and techniques to mould and make a thing of beauty.

This book is primarily about formation: how God forms us and shapes us, transforms us and reshapes us, as we take up the call to follow Jesus.

It began life when I was granted a research opportunity by the William Leech Fellowship in 2010. For a year I was freed of all other work responsibilities and, with the support of Durham University's Department of Theology and Religion, allowed to investigate the role of small groups in churches in the north-east of England (referred to in this book as 'the Leech research'). This yielded some insights that have been shared in various places, including publications,[1] but the more I pursued the research the more other questions became pressing. Many people join small groups in their church with the hope of strengthening and developing their discipleship, and an increasing number of churches expect their members to be part of a small group for the same purpose – to be formed as disciples. But how does God form and transform us? What are the vehicles of grace that enable change and growth? How do we recognize them and work with them? If small groups are important, what about those who do not want or cannot belong to such groups? These questions led me to try to locate what I was discovering about small groups in a broader theological framework that includes some understanding of the

---

1 Roger L. Walton, 'Disciples Together: The Small Group as a Vehicle for Discipleship Formation', *Journal of Adult Theological Education* 8:2 (2012), pp. 99–114, and 'Ordinary Discipleship', in Jeff Astley and Leslie Francis (eds), *Exploring Ordinary Theology*, Farnham: Ashgate, 2013, pp. 179–88.

biblical notion of formation and some reflection on Christian companionship. The book is the result of my efforts.

It is written in two distinct sections. Section 1 sets out the pattern of formation discerned in the Scriptures and particularly in the Gospels. It identifies mission, worship and intentional Christian community as primary vehicles for formation and transformation. These are the regular determinative agents in Christian disciple-ship and the normal channels of God's grace to God's people. Christian education is then considered as a derived or dependent set of tools for working with the three primary energies, and its purposes are set out, with some reflections on our current practice in relation to enquirers' courses, gathering for worship, and train-ing for ordination.

Section 2 is focused on small groups. It opens with a sociological perspective on small groups and their use (Chapter 5), followed by a historical outline of the changing role of small groups in churches across the twentieth century (Chapter 6). Chapter 7 distils the research work of various studies on church-related small groups and majors on the research of Robert Wuthnow in the USA in the mid-1990s and my own research in the north-east of England. Both these research projects highlight the tendencies towards mutual support, self-help and the privatizing of religious experiences in small groups. The last chapter in this section, Chapter 8, is an attempt to construct an approach to small groups that combines spiritual growth with a broadly based missional orientation, including engagement with issues of injustice, as well as making disciples and serving our neighbours.

Finally Chapter 9 offers the beginning of a theology of compan-ionship. My conviction, like that of the founder of Methodism, John Wesley, is that the journey of discipleship is not intended to be made alone but in the company of others. We are to be disciples together. The form this shared journeying takes is not in itself the most important point. It could be via small groups or in other forms of relationship. The key thing is that we are not alone in the journey; we need the insights, encouragement, gifts and truth-telling of others along the way. To see our calling in this way is to recognize that we, and the whole Church of God, are on the move, restless until we find our rest in God, and part of a pilgrim people seeking a kingdom that is not of the earth but in its coming transforms the world with the grace of God.

My hope is that you will find something here to help you make the journey of discipleship, if not more easily then at least more intentionally and with greater awareness. I pray that you may enter more wholeheartedly into the forming and transforming processes of God.

Roger Walton

Section 1

Formation

The four chapters that follow are all concerned with how Christian disciples are formed. The argument they attempt to make can be stated quite simply. Chapter 1 argues that it is by participating in mission that disciples are formed. Chapter 2 considers worship and outlines the ways participation in worship forms worshippers. Chapter 3 focuses on Christian community as a forming agent and explores the role of intentional Christian communities for forming disciples. These three, I suggest, are the primary formative agents of Christian disciples. As following Jesus into the work of the kingdom, worshipping God and living out faith in community are the essence of Christian faith, they are also the main means through which disciples are formed in God's image and become Christlike.

Chapter 4 looks at the role of Christian education. In the light of the first three chapters, I contend that Christian education is a secondary not a primary source for forming disciples, and that the work of Christian education is derived from and dependent on the primary forces of mission, worship and community. Its role is to connect mission, worship and community and make bridges between these elemental energies to deepen understanding, reinforce practice and strengthen action. Seen in this light, Christian education has a sharper focus and a more urgent imperative.

I offer an agenda for Christian education in Chapter 4 that majors on three principal roles:

Working with the rhythm of discipleship:

- to help people learn and use the language of faith;
- to offer opportunities for reflection;
- to develop core and critical skills.

Building the body:

- to enable meeting;
- to nurture hospitality;
- to connect the church.

Extending and enhancing mission, worship and community:

- to enable honest appraisal;
- to draw on the tradition;
- to generate new knowledge.

At the end of Section 1 some reflections are offered on how the Church can strengthen its work for forming disciples.

Section 1 and its four main chapters constitute the groundwork for Section 2. When we come to exploring the role of small groups we will bring to that task fundamental ideas about formation, thus providing some measure of objectivity about the small-group experience. This will in turn enable us to consider the place and role of small groups in formation.

I

Forming Christian Disciples: Mission

As Jesus passed along the Sea of Galilee, he saw Simon and his brother Andrew casting a net into the lake – for they were fishermen. And Jesus said to them, 'Follow me and I will make you fish for people.' And immediately they left their nets and followed him.

Mark 1.16–18

Mark's Gospel gives us an extremely short account of the call of the first disciples. Among the four Gospel writers, Mark is known for his brief, terse, almost hurried narrative. He writes as if there is special urgency to his story, a need to tell that will not wait. Like a dying man trying to complete a story to those gathered before his time runs out, or a women who has raced up the hill with news that must be communicated, even if she has not yet got her breath back, Mark begins as he means to go on, cutting out the non-essentials to get the tale told. He does not have time, it seems, to fill in the details or answer the questions we would like to put, such as: Did Jesus know Simon (Peter) and Andrew before this day? Had they talked or worked or done business together, when Jesus was a carpenter, perhaps building boats? Had the brothers heard of Jesus before? Did he have a reputation already? What was the reaction of their families to this strange event? What happened to the business, the nets and the boat? Mark answers none of these questions; rather, in three short sentences he conveys the life-changing drama that took two fishermen and altered the course of their lives forever.

This is not, however, a disadvantage to us as readers, for Mark, by his concise style, allows us to go straight to the heart of the matter. More important than all the surrounding details for Mark is what it means to be a Christian disciple – here we have it in a nutshell.

To be a disciple is to be called by Jesus

The initiative is with Jesus. He it is who spots the two brothers and makes the invitation. Meeting with Jesus and hearing his invitation to follow is the beginning of discipleship.

To be a disciple is to follow Jesus

The invitation is as simple as it can be. 'Follow me', says Jesus – go where I go, watch what I do, listen to what I say, share my life and work, come after me on the journey I am making. This is a simple summons, even if it is abrupt and unexpected. Yet it is the heart of the message that Mark wants to convey. All through the second Gospel Jesus is ahead, and the disciples are to follow. This is not just a simple relating of what happened as they trudged through Galilee and Samaria and Jerusalem, namely that Jesus was out front, it is a message about every disciple's call.

Before the days of satnavs, sometimes a car driver would be asked to follow someone else's car to get to a location. Many of us know what that meant: trying to keep up and not lose sight of the leading car at traffic lights or junctions where you have to stop as another car, or worse still a series of cars, including a large lorry, move in between. Getting in the right lanes at the right times for the turns depends on catching sight of the car and its indicator lights. With proper focus on your driving and the traffic around, you have to make sure you can see what the leader is doing and try to do the same. This is the thrust of Mark's narrative. Disciples are to keep their eyes on Jesus who is ahead, and follow him.[1]

At the end of Mark's Gospel the angel encountered in the empty tomb reminds the disciples of the first call. The angel says:

> Do not be alarmed; you are looking for Jesus of Nazareth, who was crucified. He has been raised; he is not here. Look, there is the place they laid him. But go, tell his disciples and Peter that

---

[1] Ernest Best, *Disciples and Discipleship: Studies in the Gospel According to Mark*, Edinburgh: T. & T. Clark, 1986.

he is going ahead of you to Galilee; there you will see him, just as he told you. (Mark 16.6–7)

Notice that the words 'follow me', though not repeated in this angelic pronouncement, are nevertheless implicit in the passage. For although Jesus is not speaking to the disciples directly, his summons hangs invitingly in the air. Once again the disciples are being summoned by Jesus to follow. Jesus, says the angel, will go before them to Galilee, where, if they follow, they will see him. The journey of following Jesus, which Mark has so graphically and urgently told, up to Jesus' death, is not yet over. It continues. Those who hear the voice of Jesus, echoed in the words of the angel, are invited to follow him again into mission and transformation.

To be a disciple is to be changed

The summons is simply to follow. Yet, what Jesus says next reveals what will happen if Simon and Andrew choose to take up the challenge. They will be changed. The words 'I will make you fish for people' points to two features of this calling. First, 'I will make you …' is a promise of transformation. Being in the company of Jesus will entail a radical makeover of mind, heart and lifestyle, and those who make this journey will never be the same again. Second, the words 'fish for people' indicate that the way to new life will be through participating in the mission of God. Experience and skill to date, as fishermen, will be relocated in the work of the kingdom – for Mark has told us in the preceding verse that Jesus' message was about the good news of the kingdom of God (1.15). In other words, if they take up this call they will begin a journey that will change them for good because they will be caught up in God's extraordinary ways as they touch human life and society. Later on we will see that this kingdom is to be found in the towns and cities of their region, at dinner parties and in deserts, in the mundane and the miraculous, among the kind and open but also among the poor, the ill and the outcast, with both Jews and Gentiles, on high mountains and in lonely places and ultimately in the experience of death on a cross. But for now these would-be disciples are not told this. They are simply told they will be changed in the mission work of God, and they are invited to follow Jesus.

To be a disciple means to let go

Again Mark captures a trait of discipleship in a stark and arresting way: 'immediately they left their nets and followed him'. He wants his readers to understand the all-encompassing nature of responding to the call of Jesus. It is not an add-on, nor an optional, spare-time activity; it is costly and demanding and requires a full and total response. Mark knows that those who followed Jesus, both among the early disciples and, later on, in the Christian Church, did not necessarily give up their employment, abandon their family or bestow all their goods on the poor (most did none of these), but he wants his readers to know that to follow Jesus still requires everything. There are no half measures. Following Jesus means letting go of what is familiar and affords security and trusting in the one who calls.

So here is a working definition of discipleship that we have drawn out from Mark's account of the call of Peter and Andrew: to be a disciple is to hear the call of Jesus, to take up that call and follow him, to let go of everything to engage in God's mission and be transformed in the process.

Forming and transforming disciples

If I am right, and this is the essence of discipleship for Mark, how then are disciples formed? In answering this question let us return to the words of Jesus in verse 17. When Jesus says, 'I will make you', the verb used here in Mark is the same as that used in the Greek version of Genesis for God's creating of the world: *poieō*. Although it might be pushing the translation a bit to render Mark 1.17 as 'Follow me and I will *create* you as fishers of people', being aware of this word and its usage does allow us to think about the meaning in a slightly different way. We tend to associate the idea of 'making' with the manufacture of goods or inanimate objects. Furniture is made; teapots are made; plastic and card are made, produced from raw materials via manufacturing processes. If the English word is used of men and women, it sits uneasily. We do not 'make' human beings in the same way as if they were there to be hammered into a particular shape or manipulated by heat or chemicals. For one thing, the very essence of a human being is linked to an ability to choose, to will, to respond and to resist, so any kind of 'making' without voluntary consent and cooperation is something less than respectful and not too likely to succeed.

The word, 'create', on the other hand, conveys a range of meanings that can be applied to human growth and development. There is a moment of creation when a sperm meets an egg and a human embryo is conceived. Something new and organic has begun, but like the creation it has a life of its own that will interact with its creator(s) over many years, and almost certainly manifest itself in resistance at some stage! It is a creative and responsive parent who continues to help shape her son or daughter and yet remains open to the child's individuality and developing personality. Indeed over the long term, the ability to influence and shape a person's life will depend on the quality of the relationships involved. This is surely Jesus' meaning too. His invitation to follow offers transformation through relationship with him. If Jesus is to make these fishermen into fishers of men – to use the older and better play on words – it is to be through relational engagement, not through imposed or controlling processes.

The word *poieō* is used in this passage with another linked word that means 'to become'. A more literal translation would be, 'I will make you to become fishers of people'. It is clumsy as a translation but suggests that we are not talking about an instant but a gradual change over time. The relationship to Jesus is the key to making new, but alterations will take time. In other words, the disciples will be changed gradually through their ongoing relationship with Jesus.

Another biblical word for creating or making is 'forming'. Genesis 2.7 uses this for God's activity of creating human beings:

'then the LORD God *formed* man from the dust of the ground, and breathed into his nostrils the breath of life; and the man became a living being'.[2]

The word is often used of how God relates to living things. God forms the earth (Ps. 90) and every bird and animal (Gen. 2.19) as well as human beings (Gen 2.7). God is said to form individuals in the womb (Jer. 1.5; Ps. 139.16) and individual parts of the body and the human spirit (Ps. 94.9; Zech. 12.1). Throughout the Scriptures God forms and reforms his people (Isa. 43.1, 7, 21). The invitation of Jesus to Peter and Andrew, with its promise of change, is best understood within this frame of reference: God's continuing loving relationship with his people to form them. However, in the case of Peter and Andrew the invitation is not so much to be formed – you could say that as adults and workmen they already had been at least partly formed – but rather to be transformed. Perhaps that is why Jesus plays with the word 'fishers'. By following him they will not be abandoning either their selves or the skills of their trade but rather undergoing a transformation wherein both their personalities and their abilities will be given new depth of meaning and purpose.

The idea of discipleship as being transformed by the relationship with God through Christ seems to be echoed into the Early Church. When Paul is writing to the Christians in Rome he suggests that the Christian calling is to be 'transformed by the renewing of your minds' (Rom. 12.2), and when he writes to the Christians in Corinth he puts it like this:

> And all of us, with unveiled faces, seeing the glory of the Lord as though reflected in a mirror, are being transformed into the same image from one degree of glory to another. (2 Cor. 3.18)

So we might say the path of discipleship is a journey of transformation. God works in and with those who take up the invitation to follow Jesus to change them, shaping them and moulding them for his purpose and for their fulfilment as human beings.

---

2 The main word used for formation in the Scriptures is the Greek *plassō*, found mostly in the LXX and corresponding to the Hebrew *yartsar*.

If God is active in transforming human beings and the sum-mons to follow Jesus is an invitation into a transformational process, this is an exciting prospect. Most of us want to be different, better, more thoughtful and kind, more patient and loving, more calm and self-controlled. We want to fulfil our potential, discover other, deeper parts of ourselves, to develop new abilities and become more fully alive. So this is an attractive offer, but how will this transformation take place?

Mission as the primary location of formation

Change will occur as we engage in mission. This is certainly the intention for the disciples in the invitation offered by Jesus in Mark's account. The call into the work of the kingdom is clearly intended. Verse 15 has set the scene. Jesus has recently taken up this calling himself and immediately calls others into the work with him. What the kingdom of God means, however, is yet to be fully set out. This will become much clearer in the places into which the disciples will follow Jesus.

Where are the disciples taken? According to Mark the first stop is Capernaum, where they listen to Jesus teaching – though we are not told what he taught – and then see him heal people living with a variety of illnesses. Across Galilee they continue to be among the sick, and then eat at the home of a tax collector – many saw tax collectors as the real traitors of the time! All this is more like an action movie than an initiation into a philosophy. Before Mark 4 we do not get to find out much about Jesus' ideas. He does not offer any structured teaching but rather responds to the comments of others on his actions. The main stress of chapters 1—3 is on doing, and Jesus' actions speak loudly about healing, forgiveness, compassion and inclusion. After a few parables about the nature of God's kingdom (4.1–32), the disciples follow Jesus again to some more challenging and uncomfortable places: into a storm (4.35); among the deeply disturbed (5.1); to those facing the death of their child and to a woman excluded from physical contact with others for 12 years (5.21). Finally they return with Jesus to his home town of Nazareth, where people are sceptical and he is rejected. Despite the thin teaching content up to this point, Jesus sends his disciples on a mission where they do what they have seen Jesus doing: proclaim the kingdom, heal the sick and cast out demons. On returning they face the reality of the cruel world they inhabit as they hear about the death of John the Baptist and then follow Jesus into another set of discomfort zones: among the hungry (6.30, cf. 8.1); confronting fear at the dead of night (6.45); facing the conflict with critics (7.1–7); dealing with demanding foreigners (7.24–30).

It is true that after Mark 8, as Jesus turned towards Jerusalem, he teaches more, but the teaching arises almost always out of particular encounters (with children at 8.10–13; would-be followers at 10.17 and disputes about who is greatest at 10.35) or in relation to places that they go (a high mountain 9.2–13; Jerusalem and the Temple from 11.1).

There can be little doubt that the places into which the disciples follow Jesus and the people they meet are central to their learning and transformation. It is here, where the poor, the disturbed and the sick live or where children appear, where ambition is exposed or conflict faced, that formation occurs. Discipleship in Mark is mission-shaped.

It is said of Óscar Romero that while he was a good and able priest and a careful servant of his Church, he was largely unaware of the plight of the poor in El Salvador until he moved to be Bishop of Santiago de María in 1974. It was there he encountered the repression of the rural workers. He became alert to the violence and injustice under which people lived as he met them on his visits, and then as he opened his rectory and diocesan building to shelter the dispossessed. This led him to a better understanding of the reality they lived.[3] On his installation as archbishop in 1977 he found himself more exposed to the oppression of the poor and became outspoken and critical of the authorities, until on 24 March 1980 he was assassinated as he presided at

---

3 Marie Dennis, Renny Golden and Scott Wright, *Oscar Romero: Reflections on His Life and Writings*, Modern Spiritual Masters Series, Maryknoll, NY: Orbis Books, 2000, p. 9.

Mass. Widely regarded as a saintly man, Romero put down his transformation to the places into which he followed Jesus. At a conference towards the end of his life he reflected as follows:

> I am going to speak to you simply as a pastor, as one who, together with his people, has been learning the beautiful but harsh truth that the Christian faith does not cut us off from the world but immerses us in it, that the church is not a fortress set apart from the city. The church follows Jesus who lived, worked, struggled and died in the midst of a city, in the polis.[4]

When Matthew sets out for us a much more organized presentation of Jesus' teaching, he begins the first block of teaching with the Sermon of the Mount. The opening of the Sermon is a series of blessings. At first reading this appears to be a set of declarations of God's favour on certain unexpected groups – the poor in spirit, those mourning for loved ones, the meek, the persecuted and those longing for justice. But these blessings carry an invitation even as they are listed. They call all who hear of God's blessing to visit those places to know its reality. Charles Elliott's evocative translation of the word 'blessed' as 'you are in the right place' captures this well.[5]

> You are in the right place among the poor in spirit, for theirs is the kingdom of heaven.
> You are in the right place alongside those who mourn, for they will be comforted.
> You are in the right place with the meek, for they will inherit the earth.
> You are in the right place when you hunger and thirst for righteousness, for you will be filled.
> You are in the right place among the merciful, for they will receive mercy.

---

4 Dennis et al., *Oscar Romero*, p. 16.
5 Charles Elliott, *Praying the Kingdom: Towards a Political Spirituality*, London: Darton, Longman & Todd, 1985.

You are in the right place among the pure in heart, for you will see God.

You are in the right place working with peacemakers, for they will be called children of God.

You are in the right place when you are persecuted for righteousness' sake, for there is the kingdom of heaven.

You are in the right place when people revile you and persecute you and utter all kinds of evil against you falsely on my account. Rejoice and be glad, for your reward is great in heaven, for in the same way they persecuted the prophets who were before you.[6]

The message is the same as that in the invitation of Jesus to Peter and Andrew recorded in Mark 1. It is when you go into these places in the company of Jesus that you are blessed, for there you are in the right place to discover God and be transformed.

The challenge to go to places outside our comfort zones is one way of expressing the transforming dynamic of God's kingdom. It is also possible to see it in another way. Many of the places into which Jesus took his disciples were everyday, familiar places and experiences – having a meal in a home, attending a wedding, going up to a festival, visiting the Temple – and it would be unusual to visit any of these without encountering the poor or disadvantaged on the way. It might be that the disciples were not so much taken to new places as enabled to see familiar places through fresh eyes – as sites of epiphany and blessing where God was not absent but especially present. Being with Jesus in these familiar places was an invitation to see differently and act differently.

For me mission is both. Sometimes it is finding the courage to go to the uncomfortable place – such as setting out for the first time with street angels into the night-time economy with its binge drinkers and tendency to antisocial and violent behaviour, or choosing to stand alongside those threatened by racist rallies in our cities or trying to share a word of faith in a hostile atmosphere. At other times mission is simply being among my family

---

6 This is my translation using Elliott's idea.

and local community, commuting to work, having a holiday or attending a neighbourhood street party and recognizing that these places may be holy also – a source of both blessing and challenge, a site of God's kingdom. In both experiences of mission I am confronted with the invitation to see through the eyes of Jesus, and in seeing differently, to act differently.

According to Mark's account we are formed as we engage in mission, whatever form it takes.

Vital ingredients

Some recipes can be successful with a few ingredients left out but some change dramatically. A friend told me that as a student he had decided to make a semolina pudding for his flatmates when it was his turn in the kitchen. In his desire to do it well he worked hard. He gathered the milk, caster sugar, butter and even grated nutmeg to create a good flavour. He followed the instructions for making the dessert carefully, but forgot to use the semolina! It was eatable, he said, but in no way was it a semolina pudding.

Clearly, according to Mark's Gospel mission is a vital ingredient – in any account of the formation of disciples, you cannot leave it out. It is in and through mission that we are changed by our encounters with others, for it is often in them that we meet the 'otherness' of God. But at the same time Christian mission cannot be a transforming process if we leave out the Christ part. The essential ingredient in the formation of Christian disciples is a relationship with the living Christ. The disciples were involved in mission, and they lived in community together with all the challenges this brought, but all that would not have formed them as true followers of Jesus were he not with them. The good news they were proclaiming was present in the person of Jesus. In him they met its reality. Because he accompanied them in mission to open their eyes, they could see; because he lived with and taught them in community, they knew it was possible to live in a new way; because he modelled for them what it meant to be a servant, they themselves could leave old notions and patterns behind and learn to put others first. It was in Jesus that the kingdom of God itself was seen and known. The disciples' relationship to the one they followed was vital for their formation.

And in this relationship they kept having to return to that very first experience of leaving things behind. Mark tells that Simon and Andrew 'left everything' to follow. But this was only the beginning. The symbolic leaving behind of boats and nets is met again and again in their experience of travelling with Jesus. They have to leave places where they have been popular (Mark 6.45) or had divine illumination (9.8), and exchange territories of relative safety for places of danger (10.32). Most of all they have to let go of established ideas that have formed their world view up to this point: that the wealthy were blessed by God; that greatness lies in power over others; that men rather than women and children were the ones to show the way to God; that victory would never involve humiliation and suffering. All these notions would be challenged along the way, and the disciples would be invited over and over again to let go and follow.

Learning to let things go, especially views of how the world is, would appear to be one of the hardest things we ever have to do, especially as adults. John Hull has argued that adults have often 'invested more time and more energy in being right and have more to lose in being found to be wrong'.[7] Continually meeting situations where one has to make radical changes to one's thinking sets up strong cognitive dissonance and discomfort. Yet Jesus, it seems, draws us into mission as a way of reassessing and releasing those attitudes and actions that are not in line with God's ways. In mission we act ourselves into new ways of thinking, wherein we can let go of old ideas and ways. And as many who have experienced great loss will testify, letting go can be the key to new life and personal transformation.

---

7 John M. Hull, *What Prevents Christian Adults from Learning?*, London: SCM Press, 1985, p. 101.

Summary

This chapter has argued that a primary site for the formation of disciples is mission. Following Mark's account we see that the invitation to follow Jesus was one into an adventure of God's work in the world. This involved doing and seeing differently as the disciples sought to keep their eyes on Jesus up ahead and were willing to leave behind lifestyles that did not match the unfolding character of the God they were discovering. It is in this missionary endeavour, as they go to new places with Jesus or visit familiar places and see them differently, that they are being formed, reformed and transformed.

In the next chapter we will look at another powerful source of Christian formation, namely worship. For a second great wellspring of transformation is to be found in the worshipping community.

2

Forming Christian Disciples: Worship

Now at the time of the incense-offering, the whole assembly of the people was praying outside. Then there appeared to him an angel of the Lord, standing at the right side of the altar of incense.

Luke 1.10–11

In the previous chapter we looked at the call of the disciples at the beginning of Mark's Gospel and were immediately taken into a narrative about mission. Had we started with the Gospel of Luke we would have found ourselves beginning in a different place. For after the foreword about why and how Luke has come to write his account (Luke 1.1–4), Luke takes us immediately to the Temple, where worship is going on and where a certain priest, named Zechariah, is offering incense. It is in the context of worship, when everyone is praying, that Zechariah encounters an angel, and it is this revelation in worship that sets the whole story going.

The Temple is an important site in Luke's Gospel. In the very last verse of the book the disciples are found in the Temple continually blessing God (Luke 24.53). So it would be fair to say that Luke's account of the good news and discipleship begins and ends in worship.

In this chapter we will argue that a second primary place of formation is worship: disciples are formed in and by worship.

Worshipping God

As one of my college tutors regularly reminded those of us training to lead worship, worship is a transitive verb. Worship always has an object. We do not worship; rather, we worship God. God is the focus and addressee of our worship. Those gathered to worship offer praise, thanks and adoration to God, they confess to God and they ask God for guidance and help. This notion is not confined to Christian worship – it could be applied to most world faiths. Worshippers, individually and corporately, open their hearts and minds, their lives and their experience to the one who transcends and is beyond all things, in the belief that God hears them and desires in some form to interact with them.

It may seem strange, therefore, to speak of worship as an agent of formation, as if in the forming of disciples we are somehow to employ worship for an end other than that of worshipping God. But it is precisely because worship is orientated to God that formation is not only possible but to be expected. There are a number of reasons for this. First, as James Smith has effectively argued, we become like the things we most love and desire.[1] You see it in long-term married couples, enduring friendship, even in those who love their pets. Over a period of time the love expressed from one to the other leads to the adoption of mannerisms, views and ways of acting. It is not that one loses identity but that love for another shapes and moulds, so that in some way we reflect the one who is the object of our care and attention. Thus in worship our attentiveness to God and our expressions of love towards the divine are inevitably shaping who we are.

Second, as we suggested in the previous chapter, God is continually active in forming the created order and all creatures within it. Thus at a moment of openness to God, which worship represents, God's grace has a special opportunity to form and transform us. Again according to Luke, these transforming encounters are regularly experienced by worshippers in the Acts of the Apostles as the Spirit becomes the empowering agent of worship, infusing the gathered community with new life and changing their perceptions and actions (Acts 2.1–4; 4.23–31; 10.44–8; 13.2). The very essence of worship is transformative.

---

1 James K. A. Smith, *Desiring the Kingdom: Worship, Worldview, and Cultural Formation*, Grand Rapids, MI: Baker Academic, 2009.

Forming the people of God in worship

So how does this work? How does worship form disciples?

Worship places us within a larger narrative

Christian worship takes many forms, from silent contempla-
tion, through the high rhetoric of preaching and exuberant
singing, to carefully crafted eucharistic liturgies. It can happen
in small, plain chapels, ornate cathedrals, large preaching halls,
borrowed or rented rooms or even in the open air. (One of my
most treasured memories of worship is an Easter-morning sun-
rise service at Kinver Edge in the West Midlands, when the sun
seemed to burst into the sky and suddenly illuminate a massive
landscape previously hidden in the darkness.) What all these have
in common is that they place the individual experience and story
in a larger frame. The sense that there is a bigger picture may be
conveyed in many ways: by stained-glass windows and vast space
in cathedrals; by telling the story of salvation through preaching;
by the rich poetic language of liturgy or hymns; by the stillness
and silence of Quaker meetings. However it is communicated, the
very nature of worship is to place the finite creature alongside the
eternal and transcendent, and this in turn causes us to reflect on
who we are and who we might be.

It is said that the former US President Franklin D. Roosevelt
used to have a little ritual with the famous naturalist, William
Beebe. After an evening's discussion the two men would go outside and look into the night sky. Gazing at the stars, they would
find the lower left-hand corner of the great square of Pegasus.
One of them would then recite these words as part of the ritual:
'That is a spiral galaxy of Andromeda. It is as large as our Milky
Way. It is one of a hundred million galaxies. It is 750,000 light
years away. It consists of 100 billion suns, each larger than our
sun.' They would then pause, and Roosevelt would finally say:
'Now I think we feel small enough. Let us go to bed!'

Worship places us in a similar frame, but the effect of locating
our story inside a much bigger one is not always to make us feel

small or insignificant but often to inspire, to encourage and to prompt action as, in that divine perspective, we consider what we might do and be to serve God. How God is portrayed and understood in this context will, of course, determine whether our response is to forgive our neighbour, campaign for an end to child poverty and offer to be involved with the homeless or take up arms to destroy 'enemies'. Either way it is clear that placing our story within a larger one has the power to form and transform us.

Worship engages us in meaning-making

Robert Cotton tells a story about the chapel and monastery built on the site of the theatre just outside the city of Verona. This ancient theatre was distinct from the amphitheatre at the centre of the city where the gladiatorial games and popular entertainment took place, in that the purpose of this theatre on the edge of town was to explore meaning. To go to this theatre was, he says, to seek a deeper understanding of life: 'this is the venue for meaning, this is where politics happen – speeches that tell us who we are or persuade us to be more than we already are. This is where presentations are made that challenge, correct or judge our behaviour.' It is 'a place, not of make-believe but of "make real"'. To have built a church on this site is appropriate, says Cotton, for the church is the natural successor to this theatre in Verona – it too is a place of meaning-making.[2]

I like this story. It nicely captures an important aspect of the experience of worship, namely that worship is an arena of meaning-making: it prompts us to make sense of our lives and to engage in reflection. This may be at the cognitive level of rational thought solicited and aided by preaching. Equally, meaning may be evoked at a more subterranean level by music, symbol, liturgy and architecture. The worship setting is conducive to that natural impulse of human beings to make meaning.

---

2 Robert Cotton, *Reimagining Discipleship: Loving the Local Community*, London: SPCK, 2012, pp. 20–1.

Bridget Nichols points out that the meaning worshippers make may often be unorthodox in the sense that it does not necessarily conform to the official doctrine. She tells the story of a woman who, inspired to pray in a redecorated Lady Chapel, reported that it made her feel 'sanctuous'. It was for the woman a positive word, but was in all probability invented by the mistaken remembrance of words used by priests who had led worship. It seems to combine being sanctified and virtuous, indicating that it made her feel a better person for prayer.[3] For this woman, an invented word was a form of meaning-making that both articulated her experience and expressed it in theological language, albeit creatively derived from more widely understood concepts. She had made her own meaning.

I could add to this, as could many preachers, stories of people who have thanked me for something I said from the pulpit that 'helped' them but that I have no recollection of saying. What they attributed to me was not my meaning at all; rather, because people come to acts of worship seeking meaning and direction, they often make their own connections and develop their own meaning. Nichols suggests that we should not be too quick to stifle or correct these 'misunderstandings', because the encouragement of meaning-making runs with the grain of worship, and by engagement in the process, 'sometimes a more glorious understanding will result'.[4] The context of worship invites meaning-making.

To put it in more formal terms: hermeneutics are at work in worship as the horizon of our personal world view and self-understanding meets the horizon of the meaning embedded in symbols, rituals and words of worship. As we bring ourselves into the meaning-making place and its activity, new meanings begin to present themselves to us and we form new horizons of understanding for our lives and of ourselves.

---

3 Bridget Nichols, 'A Tune Beyond Us, Yet Ourselves: Ordinary Worship and Ordinary Theology', in Jeff Astley and Leslie J. Francis (eds), *Exploring Ordinary Theology: Everyday Christian Believing and the Church*, Farnham and Burlington, VT: Ashgate, 2013, p. 160.

4 Nichols, 'A Tune Beyond Us', p. 167.

Worship forms attitudes and orientation

All forms of worship contain elements of repetition. Some practices are repeated on every occasion and others over time. Most
weeks in church I am bidden to confess my sins and to join
with others in saying the Lord's Prayer. Every year we celebrate
Christmas and Easter in ways broadly predictable, even if creativity has been applied to the occasions. At Holy Communion
(Eucharist or Mass), the structure and movement at the heart of
the liturgy is generally the same each time.

Repetition plays an important part in almost all learning –
though there has been a tendency to understate this in recent years.
It enables foundational skills such as language acquisition. Just
as young children learn words initially by hearing them repeated
around them many times, so disciples learn the language of faith
by encountering it in worship. And just as children develop their
language skills by tentatively venturing into speech, so disciples
are formed as they recognize and respond, with increasing confidence, in the medium of God-talk spoken in worship. Put another
way: little by little they become functionally literate within the
community of practice that is a worshipping congregation.

But being formed in worship is more than learning the language
spoken. It also involves repeated participation in meaningful
practices and rituals. James Smith uses this approach to argue
that worship is the locus of Christian formation.[5] Positing that
we are basically creatures of desire and formed by what we love,
he applies the notion of liturgy and ritual to what seem at first
unlikely places: the shopping mall, sports event and university
campus. In each case he identifies the rituals and practices that
at once express and reinforce the concept of the good lying at the
heart of each. For example, the shopping mall is structured to
stimulate our desire for products and services and thus to form us
as consumers. We desire to be attractive, up to date and significant and to show signs of wealth, security and popularity. The
mall and its practices are designed to provide a sense of achieving

---

5 Smith, *Desiring the Kingdom*.

these things from the shopping experience. All the time we are browsing at the windows, eating in the cafes, seeing the beautiful and famous wearing designer clothes or being flattered by attendants, we are participating in rituals that nurture and strengthen a particular concept of the good (in this case that we are fulfilled when we buy and possess things), with a corresponding growth in our desire for it.

When he applies this idea to worship, he says that the rituals and practices of worship are designed to nurture our love for God – the only truly satisfying object of human desire. So when we say the Lord's Prayer, for example, we are placing ourselves in the way of the kingdom: asking that God's will be done on earth, that each has enough to live on, that we might be forgiven and be able to forgive, that we may not face trials that are too much for us or be caught up in evil. By saying this prayer again and again we are orientating ourselves in the way of Jesus and growing into the life of the kingdom.[6]

The same could be said of confession in worship: it reminds us that we are part of a fallen world that needs forgiveness and healing, and that each of us has some part in that brokenness. Likewise, when we celebrate communion we are remembering and entering into the death of Jesus. In a symbolic yet powerful way we are enacting the truth that the love of God meets destructive evil upon the cross and rises from death to draw all humanity to a feast of equals loved by God. By taking bread and wine we are aligning ourselves with that way of living. It is forming us at a deep and profound level.

Worship involves encountering difference

To worship is to associate with others, to be part of a worshipping community. While it can be argued that one can worship on one's own, and there are stories and even jokes about individuals marooned on desert islands building a church to worship in (and,

---

6 See N. T. Wright, *The Lord and His Prayer*, London: SPCK, 1996.

as one joke goes, also building a church they do not go to!), worship for most is a corporate affair. It is done alongside and with others. It arises from a community and is experienced in a community; and once there is a community there is diversity and difference, and where there is diversity and difference there is challenge.

Imagine getting an invitation to a party from God. You feel honoured that your name is written by hand on the invitation. You have been chosen to be there. Though there is no particular reason why this should be so, you are identified as a very special guest. When you get to the venue you are treated with particular respect and given individual attention, which reinforces your sense of being special. But as you look around, you realize that many of the folk summoned are people you would not have invited at all; and yet everyone there is treated in the same way, as a VIP. Moreover the way people want to enjoy the party is different from your idea of a good time. The dances, games, food and songs are not all familiar to you. Yet you are, with everyone else there, a guest at God's party. It becomes clear that if this party is going to be a great celebration, you are going to have to join in with others who are different from you as well as do some of the things you know and enjoy.

Worship draws people together in their diversity. It invites us to place ourselves in a bigger frame of reference or narrative; to work at meaning for our own lives alongside others; to make sense of why these others are here and what is our relationship to them. This becomes acute when the community has to work together on mission, church maintenance and common life – if you want to see how many diverse opinions there can be in a worshipping community, propose a change at church council! There is in worshipping communities, as in all communities, the natural and inevitable clash of personalities, politics and power struggles. Yet the words of the Scripture, often proclaimed in the liturgy, affirm that 'we who are many (= different) are one body, for we all partake of the one bread' (1 Cor. 10.17).

Encountering difference poses a challenge to a worshipping community. People may grow to embrace others different from themselves and find ways of including and respecting each other, or they may resist change, use power to close doors and make the Church in their own image. British church history in the last 50 years demonstrates what happens when Christian immigrants come to UK churches and get a cold reception. Instead of multi-ethnic congregations enriched by a great variety of styles of worship, it led to people feeling rejected and multiple churches springing up. This is not new – the early Christians struggled with it too. The New Testament shows that difference and diversity put a stain on the worshipping communities (see for example Paul's letters to the Corinthians or note the underlying tensions of the letters of John.) But where difference is embraced and worked with, it can form us positively.

Not long ago I was to lead a Covenant Service in a church in Bradford. A few days before the service the minister warned me there would two new families in the congregation who spoke no English. They had very recently come from the (African Republic of) Congo. Some spoke French, some Swahili, she told me. Could I do something to include them? On the internet I managed to find how to say 'Good morning and welcome' in Swahili, and so at least I welcomed everyone in three languages. How good my pronunciation was I am not sure, but it occasioned smiles and genuine warmth because I had tried. Otherwise I do not think the service was particularly geared to these newcomers. Afterwards I noticed how well the congregation included the strangers. They ensured that adults and children had drinks and chocolate, and I saw several attempting to communicate in very rusty French or through body language. There were lots of smiles and laughter. Within a month the Sunday School staff had started to do Bible stories with lots of visuals and bold ventures into unknown languages. The minister told me that the best bit was when the Sunday School joined the congregation towards the end of each worship service to relate what they had been doing in their separate activity, and children and adults corrected each other's Swahili, French and English! It was clear to me that all involved in this experience – newcomers and long-established members – were being changed as they sought to worship together.

This is a story of embracing difference in a very multicultural city. But even where a church is seemingly monochrome, people are diverse, their personalities differ and the differences pose a challenge. Any group worshipping together will encounter difference and must make theological as well as practical sense of how they are together. Whether the responses to the challenge are positive or negative, they will shape how people see themselves and others. Engagement with difference is formative for disciples, and it is always present in worshipping communities.

Worship as openness to God's grace

All the above are different ways of saying that worship opens us to the grace of God. In worship it is possible to be formed and transformed because it provides a setting in which we can place our story in a bigger frame, engage in meaning-making, enter and practise the values and attitudes of the Christian faith and engage with difference. These are all present and potent forces implicit in worship, but none guarantees our formation to be Christlike or, perhaps more accurately, they do not determine of themselves into what kind of Christian we will be formed. There are other factors that play a part in this formational process, some of which we will look at in the next chapter. For now I propose a theological point: that in worship individuals and communities encounter the grace of God.

This is a distinctively Christian theological point. It might be possible to demonstrate that there is some psychological basis for arguing that the four previously identified factors possess at least the potential to form participants, but the assertion of meeting God's grace in worship comes from a faith conviction. Grace lies at the heart of the Christian message. It is the free, unmerited, undeserved, overflowing love of God; it is the transforming power that flowed in through the life of Jesus feeding the hungry, healing the sick, forgiving sins and giving unlikely people a new start. This is the same love that comes to meet us as we gather to worship. John Wesley called worship an instituted means of grace, meaning that worship is identified in the Scriptures as a reliable place to meet the grace of God. For those who come to worship openly and honestly, willing to set their lives in a larger frame, explore meaning, enter into faith practices and engage with those different from themselves, grace is ready to draw them deeper into God's purpose and will.

I have recently returned from visiting the Corrymeela community in Northern Ireland, which since 1965 has been bringing people together from deeply divided parts of Northern Ireland to find common humanity and become committed to reconciliation. There are wonderful stories of transformation and change that have been witnessed over the years at Corrymeela. Its worship, however, is surprisingly simple and uncomplicated: 15 minutes in the morning and the same in the evening, with undemanding songs and prayer, periods of silence and an occasional liturgy built around a meal. It lacks the creativity of Iona or the drama of Taizé, yet here in these acts of worship people are changed. It is extraordinary that young people and adults who have travelled to the community thinking they are unable to sit or talk with those from the 'other' community discover, over a few days, that they have much in common, that they can pray and praise together and in the process are renewed in their vision of themselves and God. Transformation does not depend on the worship being exciting or different; rather, it is the willingness to live together for a few days, engage with each other and go to worship together, increasingly open to others and God, that works miracles of transformation. It was for me a picture of God's grace meeting people in worship and forming them as disciples.

Worship as a primary location of formation

We have argued in this chapter that worship is a primary site of formation. It is in worship that disciples are formed and transformed. Worship, like mission, is a place of encounter with God because it is a place of honesty, risk and faith, and it is a space shared with others who also have discovered Jesus and want to journey with him. These are both primary sites for discipleship formation. It is not that disciples are formed and then engage in mission and participate in worship; rather, it is precisely in doing these things that disciples are made, formed and transformed. But it is not yet the whole story. In the next chapter we will turn to the third source of formational energy: Christian community.

3

Forming Christian Disciples: Community

I give you a new commandment, that you love one another. Just as I have loved you, you also should love one another. By this everyone will know that you are my disciples, if you have love for one another.

John 13.34-5

As with Mark and Luke, the unfolding of the story of Jesus in John's Gospel is distinctive and carries its own emphases. It also gives us a particular insight into discipleship and how disciples are formed.

The opening of the Gospel is a form of high Christology, beginning the narrative in pre-history and locating the Word, the divine agent of creation, as coming to dwell among us in Jesus. This glorious poem of heaven is interwoven with the very earthy story of John the Baptist, a man sent by God to be a witness to the light coming into the world (John 1.5–6). And it is John the Baptist who as his first act of witness points some of his own disciples to Jesus, so that they leave John to join Jesus' company, to be close to Jesus and learn from him.

For John, being close to Jesus is a hallmark of a disciple. Perhaps more than the other Gospel writers, John highlights the time Jesus spends with his disciples, for as well as accompanying him on journeys and encounters they alone receive Jesus' deepest teaching in the extended section known as the final discourses. In this section (John 13—17), which covers almost a quarter of the book, Jesus repeatedly tells them that he is going away, and yet he urges them to remain close to him. They are to abide in him and he in them (15.4); if they keep his word, he and the Father will come and make their home with them (14.23) and even though he will go away, he will come again to them (15.4) and send the Spirit to be close to them and lead them deeper into the truth (16.7–14). He is the way the truth and the life – the very road to the Father (14.6). True disciples are to remain close to him. In John, the notion of the 'beloved disciple' may well act as metaphor for what it means to be a disciple – one who is intimately close to Jesus, near his heart, as at the last supper (13.23), just as Jesus is close to the Father's heart (1.18).

But equally important is for the disciples to be close to each other. It is in John's Gospel that Jesus gives a new commandment that the disciples love one another (15.15–17), and significantly, Jesus tells them this is how people will know they are his disciples: that they love one another (13.35). Just prior to this Jesus has washed their feet and called on them to do the same for each other (13.14). The commandment to love and be seen to love is set within the frame of service to one another.

This same theme of loving one another in Christian community is continued in the letters of John (1 John 2.10; 3.11; 3.23; 4.7; 4.11–12; 4.21; 2 John 1.5). Indeed it is such a strong refrain in the Johannine community that it could be their mission statement. In sharp contrast to discipleship expressed in mission or worship, among these Christians it is the quality of community that points to Jesus. To be formed as a disciple is to be formed in a community that remains close to Christ and whose members love one another.

This chapter is about the third formational energy: Christian community.

Community as a site of formation

It is undeniable that communities exert huge influence over those who belong to them. You only have to think of our families, school experience or workplaces to recognize the influence of the communities we belong to or pass through. Peer pressure and community culture form us profoundly, from the way we speak and the clothes we wear to the values we carry and how we act. Even if we are ill at ease in these communities or rebel against them, we are nevertheless shaped by them. We do not need the underpinnings of social psychology to know that inter-action in community affects us – communities are natural sites of formation.

But *how* communities affect this formation is debated among social psychologists. The insights I find most helpful come from situated learning theory and a combination of social learning theory and social constructivism.

Situated learning theory[1] emphasizes the idea that all learning is situated in particular physical and social contexts and is related to the social interaction and physical activity in which the learning occurs. Any setting – family, college, church or the NHS – can be viewed as a 'community of practice' in which people over time learn to participate. Like an apprentice, newcomers absorb the nature of the community, its purpose and activity by social interaction with members of that community and by utilizing the learning resources available within it. Participation in the com-munity provides language, insight and skill and accesses its values and power structure. Crucially, knowledge in this theory is seen not as an 'abstract entity that resides in the heads of individuals'[2] but rather as a practical capability for interacting, doing and making that is learned in a particular setting. It is social in nature and learned by participating. Thus the community's life, rhythm and practices are formative for those who engage in them.[3] A community of practice with its complex life, structure and pattern of working is a powerful shaper of people, drawing participants into its ethos, values and activities as they share in it. Whether

1 Jean Lave and Etienne Wenger, *Situated Learning: Legitimate Peripheral Participation*, Learning in Doing: Social, Cognitive, and Computational Per-spectives, Cambridge: Cambridge University Press, 1991.

2 Hans Gruber et al., 'Situated Learning and Transfer: Implications for Teaching', in P. Murphy (ed.), *Learners, Learning and Assessment*, London: Paul Chapman, 1999, pp. 215–16.

3 R. T. Putnam and H. Borko, 'What Do New Views of Knowledge and Thinking Have to Say About Research on Teacher Learning?', *Educational Researcher* 29:1 (2000), pp. 4–15.

they realize it or not, people are assimilated into its life and, by their interaction with the community, locate themselves and their sense of self within it.

Social learning theory[4] and its close cousin social constructivism[5] both emphasize the cognitive and conceptual development internal to the individual. As she or he interacts with others in a particular life or learning contexts, mental dialogical processes are triggered as ideas, behaviours and skills are observed and contextual vocabulary is assimilated and/or created together with others. Significant figures (teachers, leaders and craft-experts) play a key part, especially in providing models and actions to observe, emulate and enact, but the internal dialogue (consciously or unconsciously) will simultaneously be shaping thought forms, outlooks and beliefs. In this way the individual aligns his or her own constructs to operate more easily in community and to enable effective negotiation with others in it.

Taken together these give us an idea of the power of communities for formation of their members. They socialize people into their values and practices by a combination of active participation and the individual's cognitive engagement. The forces work together powerfully to mould and fashion the members as the community lives out its life.

The issue is not *whether* church congregations will form people – all people who participate in such communities of practice over time will be formed by them – but *what* they will form in people. Equally problematic, particularly in our age, is how people participate in several communities of practice, with different values, world views and outlooks, and retain any single sense of self or view of what is ultimately true.

---

4 The originator of this theory was Albert Bandura. See A. Bandura, *Social Learning Theory*, New York: General Learning Press, 1971.

5 See Peter L. Berger and Thomas Luckmann, *The Social Construction of Reality: A Treatise in the Sociology of Knowledge*, Garden City, NY: Anchor, 1966.

Intentional Christian communities for forming disciples

This is where we need to think a little about what the Church is for and how it constitutes its life. Stanley Hauerwas has consistently argued that social ethics and Christian education are not so much tasks the Church undertakes as the essence of its life. The Church *is* a social ethic, and the Church *is* a particular form of education.[6] What he means is that the Christian community expresses its vitality and values in the way it organizes and conducts its life.

> The church is where the stories of Israel and Jesus are told, enacted and heard, and it is our conviction that as a Christian people there is literally nothing more important we can do. But the telling of the story requires that we be a particular kind of people if we and the world are to hear the story truthfully.[7]

This is a community with a very simple aim. It is one where the story of Jesus is kept alive and communicated. But this cannot be any old community of religious storytelling. It needs to be one in which the Jesus story is voiced and transmitted with authenticity. The community must itself be enlivened, challenged and convicted by the story. It must aspire both to express the truth of the story and be continually renewed in its telling.

> The story requires the formation of a corresponding community which has learned to live in a way that makes it possible for them to hear the story.[8]

Hauerwas goes on to say that this community is primarily a community of virtue:

---

6 Stanley Hauerwas, *The Peaceable Kingdom: A Primer in Christian Ethic*, London: SCM Press, 2003 and *Christian Existence Today: Essays on Church, World, and Living in Between*, Durham, NC: Labyrinth Press, 1988.

7 Hauerwas, *Peaceable Kingdom*, pp. 99–100.

8 Hauerwas, *Christian Existence Today*, p. 101.

For the church to be rather than to have a social ethic moreover means that a certain kind of people are required to sustain it as an institution across time. They must, above all, be the people of virtue – not simply any virtue, but the virtues necessary for remembering and telling the story of a crucified saviour. They must be capable of being peaceable among themselves and with the world, so that the world sees what it means to hope in God's Kingdom. Such a people do not believe that everyone is free to do whatever they will, but we are each called upon to develop our particular gifts to serve the community of faith.[9]

Almost all of Paul's correspondence with the earliest Christian communities is about the kind of lifestyles, virtues and values that are to be present in community life that is appropriate to God revealed in Christ. These communities in Corinth, Galatia, Thessalonica and Rome have already received the message of Jesus; the question now is how to establish community life and individual conduct that make a context in which the good news of Jesus is demonstrated. This is how he puts it to the Christians in Rome.

> I appeal to you therefore, brothers and sisters, by the mercies of God, to present your bodies as a living sacrifice, holy and acceptable to God, which is your spiritual worship. Do not be conformed to this world, but be transformed by the renewing of your minds, so that you may discern what is the will of God – what is good and acceptable and perfect.
>
> For by the grace given to me I say to everyone among you not to think of yourself more highly than you ought to think, but to think with sober judgement, each according to the measure of faith that God has assigned. For as in one body we have many members, and not all the members have the same function, so we, who are many, are one body in Christ, and individually we are members one of another. We have gifts that differ according to the grace given to us: prophecy, in proportion to faith;

---

9 Hauerwas, *Peaceable Kingdom*, pp. 102–3.

ministry, in ministering; the teacher, in teaching; the exhorter, in exhortation; the giver, in generosity; the leader, in diligence; the compassionate, in cheerfulness.

Let love be genuine; hate what is evil, hold fast to what is good; love one another with mutual affection; outdo one another in showing honour. Do not lag in zeal, be ardent in spirit, serve the Lord. Rejoice in hope, be patient in suffering, persevere in prayer. Contribute to the needs of the saints; extend hospitality to strangers.

(Romans 12.1–13)

This, says Paul, is the kind of community that can tell and hear the story of Jesus properly.

The same idea underlies the whole of the correspondence to the Corinthians. They are to create a community that rings true with the message they have received. Paul's words to the new Christian community at Corinth are fundamentally how to order and express their gatherings and individual actions, so that the gospel is not only celebrated by them but recognized in and communicated through them. Paul fears that in their enthusiasm and delight in the outpouring of God's Spirit they may fail to see that their corporate and personal lives need now to look more Christlike. So he works his way through a series of issues facing their church that need a response resonant with the Christian faith. Having discussed with them how they should act in relation to food, sexual relations and charismatic gifts, he turns to the 'better way' of love (1 Cor. 13). Like the community bearing John's name, Paul recognizes that a community that practises love will be the best place to announce and celebrate the story of Jesus.

This same kind of desire to order community so that it is receptive to and resonant with the story of Jesus can be seen in the pattern of the ancient monastic orders, set out, for example, in the Rule of Benedict or the Society rules of John Wesley and rediscovered in our own time in the Iona Community and other forms of new monasticism. Jürgen Moltmann's book *The Open Church* uses a similar approach for the revitalization of congregational life, arguing that Christians are called to form community together in a way that enables them to live for others, to engage with difference and to move to share in the world's suffering.[10] In this way they reflect the pattern of Jesus and add credibility to their preaching.

Here the medium is the message. A community whose life is at odds with the message it proclaims makes the story sound hollow. A community that embodies and lives out the story of Jesus in their relationships with each other amplifies and extends the good news, adding credibility and making it easier for others to hear.

One of the most seminal expressions of what an intentional Christian community looks like in its corporate expression was set out by Dietrich Bonhoeffer in his little book *Life Together*.[11] This is a slightly deceptive book. Writing against the backdrop of the rise of Nazism, on the eve of war, and in the context of a seminary to train pastors for the Confessing Church, the setting out of a pattern of communal living for the trainee ministers looks, at first sight, a little esoteric and remote from most church communities. The structure of daily prayers at morning, noon and night, with the saying of psalms, reading the Bible, sharing meals together and praying for the world is a recognizable monastic pattern most seminaries have adopted in some form or other, but it has not usually been adopted in congregational life, at least not in this intense form. The strength of the book is to be found, however, in the underlying purpose Bonhoeffer articulates for communal living. Living together is to enable people to become aware of their own weaknesses and fantasies, practise serving and truth-telling, confront and confess sin and rely more and more on the grace of God made known in the cross. The practices are to form a people that by its life communicates the gospel.

When he writes about ministries in the community, again he surprises us. For ministry here is not identified as preaching or teaching or pastoral care. Ministries that are to be exercised between Christians living together are:

---

10 Jürgen Moltmann, *The Open Church: Invitation to a Messianic Life-Style*, London: SCM Press, 1978.

11 Dietrich Bonhoeffer, *Life Together*, London: SCM Press, 1954.

- *A ministry of holding one's tongue* – a learning of self-discipline leading to less judgement and more respect for others.
- *A ministry of meekness* – not seeking your own importance but honouring your neighbour more than yourself.
- *A ministry of listening* – a careful attending to the concerns and needs of others and a willing to talk less and listen more.
- *A ministry of helpfulness* – the willingness to be interrupted, seeing those who intrude into one's personal plans as a gift of God.
- *A ministry of bearing* – respecting and guarding others' individuality, endowments, weaknesses and oddities.

The point of all this is to form individuals in this community in the virtues and pattern of Jesus, so that the communication of the message of the crucified saviour is always carried in the way the community orders and lives out its life.

This approach of trying to articulate and live by the core practices of Jesus in the Christian community is applicable to all such communities – this is not just for seminarians. The 'rules' are not rules in an absolute sense of laws or regulations that must not be broken, but patterns of relating that attempt to embody what being a Jesus community means. Christian community must be both intentional and reflexive, so that it continually seeks to be a better mirror of the truth of the gospel. The rules are a means to train ourselves together to be God's people reflecting God's character.

Bonhoeffer's context is more apposite than we think. Because Nazism was recognized by the Confessing Church as carrying and promoting values and practices contrary to Christianity, and because these were pervading the society around, even large portions of the Church, it was clear to him that people would not learn the liberating gospel truths intuitively or from the contemporary culture; rather, they needed be practised in Christian community, intentionally and intensely, or they would be submerged and eroded by the prevailing values of nationalism, anti-Semitism, racism and violence. It is not difficult to see that many of our present-day values rooted in consumerism, individualism and greed may pose the same level of insidious threat.

Churches wishing to form disciples of Jesus must be intentional in their living. The explicit, intentional pattern of Christian living in Christian communities is for all Christians. Such places are where disciples are initiated and formed.

Stories of formation in community

My children are now adults, both in their thirties, and the Christian faith continues to be important in their lives. They would call themselves followers of Jesus and both are active in church life. When we talk about their growing up, what they remember most readily about the church they belonged to are two types of experience. First is the action the church was involved in during their growing years: the campaign for Fair Trade; organized sleepouts to draw attention to the plight of the homeless; collecting money for Christian Aid and other charities; the all-age musicals – usually written by Roger Jones – telling the story of Jesus or some part of it. In all these they were involved as children and teenagers. Second, they remember the people who took an interest in them and built relationships with them, listened to and cared for them when life was a challenge. These were folk of all ages. Some were older young people whom they admired and looked up to, but many were middle-aged and elderly, who simply thought that each child – and everyone they met – was worthy of respect and being listened to. These took time to relate to them on a one-to-one basis. Of course, my children have snatches of special acts of worship, church weekends away, youth events and some particular moments of feeling that God was close and intimate. But notice that what they remember most vividly was participating in a community that lived out its life in mission and relationships. The church was not a large one, with fewer than 90 members, and it was not without its faults and limits; but because it sought to live out the story of Jesus in its community life, it was an effective sign of that story, and they caught its message.

I tell the story above first because it is in many ways the kind of intentional Christian community I have in mind. This was not an idealized church beyond our grasp; rather, it was made up of very ordinary, for the most part working, struggling families and singles, and was a shaper of its members in the way of Jesus. In seeking to be a community in which the story of Jesus could be told and heard it was a formational community for disciples. Its members would immediately recognize that they were well short of good or perfect – and there were many episodes and aspects of its life that would not have shown it in a good light. They would acknowledge as apt the image of 'earthen vessels' used by St Paul (2 Cor. 4.7), yet at the same time they knew they had a treasure at the heart of their community, and one that should be shared. And if it were to be shared they knew they needed to live as a community valuing that treasure.

Theologically speaking the community's life together opened up windows into the kingdom of God and released channels of life-transforming grace flowing from the heart of God. In their faltering ways they were and are seeking to be a community in tune with the story they were trying to pass on. As a result they were able to open a conduit for God's grace to embrace and transform those who participated in that community.

There are other Christian communities whose values and story stand out in the way they conduct their shared life. Visit a L'Arche community, for example, where people with various abilities and disabilities live together as family, following the remarkable example of Jean Vanier, and see immediately what vision of society it carries. Stay in that community for a time, participate in its life, and you will be transformed in your understanding of yourself and others. Or volunteer for work in a hospice and work alongside those who have been stirred by a vision of human dignity throughout life and in death. These are intentional communities, both built in different ways on the story of Jesus. Their lives are structured and conducted to demonstrate a view of human beings made in the image of God. What they believe to be true is also expressed in their attitudes, actions and speech towards one another. The same approach is beginning to be seen in communities that are dementia-friendly and inclusive. In these communities, none of which is restricted to Christians, the story of Jesus has a strong authenticity. Whether one belongs to the Christian, another or no faith, the inspiring and empowering of these communities with a view of what it means to be human is resonant with the life, teaching, death and resurrection of Jesus.

My conviction is that all Christian communities are to be equally intentional to form and transform human beings.

Three formational energies: mission, worship and community

In each chapter thus far I have identified a site and energy for formation. Disciples are formed by God as they take up the invitation to mission and meet God in the unlikely and challenging places of life (Chapter 1); disciples are formed by God as they enter into worship, opening themselves up to the Creator and exploring this extraordinary world of meaning-making (Chapter 2); and disciples are formed by God as they participate in authentic Christian community living in a way that allows the story of Jesus to be told and heard (Chapter 3). These are, of course, intended to work together, reinforcing and refining our perception of and response to God. Each is a channel of God's grace and, when combined, draw us into ever fresh encounters with God, which in turn nurture our true humanity and grow in us the life of Christ so that we and all things are stamped with his image and patterned in his character.[12]

It is true that different Christian communities have majored on one or two of these three to the neglect or even exclusion of the other(s). This is dangerous. Churches that concentrate solely on the experience of worship risk becoming sectarian. Churches that focus on mission alone risk becoming dislocated activists. Churches that use all their energies for creating community risk becoming cosy clubs for members only. It is only with all three working together that formation can be dynamic and fully

---

12 Ephesians 4.15 can be translated 'so that we may cause all things to grow into Christ'.

effective. To return to the analogy of glass-blowing, the creation of fine glass occurs when heat, air and water-cooling are combined by the glass-maker. One or even two of these are insufficient for the work – all are needed.

There is one further point to make, and this is where the analogy of glass-making breaks down. To form disciples, the willing and cooperative engagement of those being formed is essential.

When I was studying in the education department of a UK university, one of the lecturers responsible for teacher training related his experience of the first lecture of the term to PGCE students – those who had a degree already and were on a one-year course to prepare to be school teachers. He said he could detect a certain attitude and look on the faces of his newly arrived students that conveyed the challenge: 'Go on, do it to us! Make us teachers!' Whether true or imagined on his part, the picture is a useful one. Trainee teachers soon discover, of course, if they do not know it already, that while the staff at the college play a part, becoming teachers does not *happen to* them but rather emerges through their own involvement in practice and reflection on experience. They are active in their own formation.

Disciples likewise are formed with their cooperation and active, intentional engagement. None of the formational energies simply 'do it to us'. Formation happens in a relationship with God, the world and the people of God, and we are actors in the process. Thus it is vital that we remain open, active, reflective and co-operative; partners with God and each other in the process. And because this is a lifelong enterprise, to stay on the track requires an act of will on our part and an ongoing willingness to visit these means of grace that invite and enable transformation.

Having set out the primary energies for formation, we must turn to how the Church works with these primary energies. This I will call Christian education, for reasons that will become clear.

4

Forming Christian Disciples: Christian Education

Therefore every scribe who has been trained for the kingdom of heaven is like the master of a household who brings out of his treasure what is new and what is old.

Matthew 13.52

In the first chapter we used the thrust of Mark's Gospel as a starting point for considering the important role of mission in forming disciples. In the second we noted the significance of Temple in Luke's narrative to explore the place of worship in formation. John's Gospel focuses on community as a way of forming the pattern of Christian discipleship. By way of introducing the next theme, we turn to Matthew's Gospel, often called the teachers' Gospel because it is structured to aid and encourage learning.

Matthew gives us a clue about what he intends to share when he tells us that Magi (wise ones) from the east came seeking Jesus. The wisdom of Jesus is then set out in a pedagogic form. Matthew orders Jesus' teaching into five distinct blocks, echoing the five books of Moses, and employs a range of mnemonic techniques to make things easier to learn and remember: three illustrations of hypocrisy and piety (Matt. 6.1–18), three parables about planting and growth; seven woes on the teachers of the law and the Pharisees (Matt. 23.13–36) and seven parables in the great parable chapter of Matthew 13. These kinds of structures are familiar to teachers. Paul Minear has suggested that the Gospel is written by a teacher for teachers and that each block of teaching is a kind of manual for disciples.[1] Whatever other purposes Matthew has in

---

1 Paul S. Minear, *Matthew: The Teacher's Gospel*, Eugene, OR: Wipf & Stock, 1982.

mind in writing his Gospel, it is clear he knows how to organize his material for the sake of education.

At the end of the Gospel, in the Great Commission of chapter 28, Jesus sends his disciples out into all the world to make disciples, with the instruction that they are to teach (*didaskontes*). What they are to teach, however, is not their own ideas or views; rather, they are to instruct others to obey everything Jesus has commanded. They are to be the scribes – those who faithfully carry and transmit to others what they have learned.

For Matthew, the truly mature disciple is pictured in 13.52. In this saying of Jesus, unique to this Gospel, the 'scribe who has been trained for the kingdom' has the ability to integrate new and old. Of course, in Matthew's church integrating old and new was much to do with being able to join together the Jewish traditions of Moses and the new truths of Jesus, so that together they might better enable people to know God. But the notion has wider application. For all disciples in every age, the ability to discern treasure, to be open to the new and to integrate the new with the old provide the dynamic at the heart of growth.

This chapter is about the role of Christian education in the forming of disciples.

Christian education – a secondary source for formation

It is important to recognize that Christian education is a secondary source for formation. It does not of itself form disciples. It may introduce, inform and extend understanding but if it is not drawing on and working with the experience of disciples in mission, worship and community it will be ineffective. Disciples cannot be formed if these primary energies are absent in their ongoing experience. Mission, worship and community are of the essence of the Christian faith and are learned by participation. Thus Christian education is dependent on the prior commitment of the Church to the core activities of mission, worship and community and only in a living relationship with these activities can it do its work.

Take the analogy of swimming. It is possible to learn what swimming is, and why it is helpful to learn to swim, in a classroom. You can also learn about buoyancy and what strokes have proved useful to human swimmers, such as breaststroke, backstroke and front crawl. But graduating from such a class does not make you a swimmer, let alone an accomplished one. Swimming can only be properly learned by getting in the water and swimming. It may take lots of trial and error and a few mouthfuls of unwanted water, but swimming will be learned in the pool, lake or sea. Because worshipping, sharing God's mission and living in Christian community define what it means to be a Christian, being formed can only take place as we are engaged in these primary callings.

This is not to say that Christian education is unimportant or optional. As it derives its work from the triple axes of mission, worship and community, it has the power to strengthen and extend our ability to participate in and even to be critical of each, so as to challenge and change our practices and more faithfully live out the calling to follow Christ. When harnessed to the three formative energies, Christian education provides ways of deepening discipleship at every stage of the journey. To return to the swimming analogy: good swimmers will be formed by swimming and lots of it, but competitive swimmers will probably also have a coach, whose job it is to help them develop their technique, fitness, stamina and performance. A good coach will employ various techniques such as observation and feedback, pay attention to particular elements such as starting drive or final touch, make sure their swimmer goes to the gym, watches videos of races and studies other swimmers' methods and strategies. Appropriate learning optimizes both practice and performance.

What is Christian education?

In this context Christian education is the planned, purposeful provision of learning opportunities to support the formation of disciples and to strengthen the life and work of the Church. It includes a range of formal and informal teaching and learning methods and various structures for individual and corporate learning. Centred on the practice of Christian living, it is to be distinguished from learning about Christianity and religious education. These are valid forms of education but geared towards different outcomes. Both aim at understanding in the cognitive sense of holding facts and concepts to be able to comprehend religion. Christian education, as understood here, is directed towards faithful Christian living and thus involves learning at cognitive, affective and practical levels. It aims at shaping the whole of a person for being a follower of Christ.

It is also important to get away from the notion that Christian education is for children or young people. There was a time when talk of education in the church context meant what the Sunday School did in its separate classes or, if there were church schools in the locality, what went on there. The Christian education we are advocating is for all and is lifelong. It does not come to an end any more than the call to discipleship comes to an end this side of death, though it may take different forms at different stages.

Most Christians are already doing it in some way – reading a book on faith, attending a Lent group or Bible study, listening to a sermon, watching a video from Christian Aid, taking part in a safeguarding day, trying out new ways of praying at the 24/7 event. Christian education will include all these kinds of activities and much more. Everything from a day course to introduce the Bible to people who have never read it before, through structured programmes to certificated courses comes under this remit. Its basic meaning is learning that will help us be better Christians.

How does Christian education help to form disciples?

We have already indicated some of the ways mission, worship and community form disciples. Christian education can enhance and strengthen this formational work in a variety of ways. For the sake of ease of communication I will set out the work of Christian education as three core tasks.

Task 1: Working with the rhythm

Disciples live a go-between life. They gather to worship God and share in community, disperse to engage with God at work in the life of the world, then gather again. Because this gathering and dispersing is regular and frequent it forms a rhythm. Elsewhere I have written of this as a spiritual rhythm at the heart of discipleship.[2] It has two loci: meeting God in the life of the Church and meeting God in the life of the world; and it is best visualized as a figure of eight (see Figure 1).

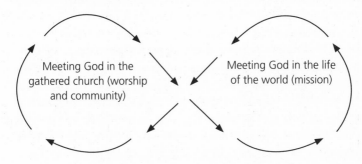

Meeting God in the gathered church (worship and community)

Meeting God in the life of the world (mission)

Figure 1: The rhythm of discipleship

Christian education works with this rhythm. It is an enabling agent to relate the two spheres of Christian experience to each other. Its interests are how best to enable people to discern God in each place of encounter, how to reflect on experience and how to translate learning from one place to the other. This will involve a number of connected pieces of work.

Language work

At base level, Christian education should be geared to helping people feel at ease with the language of faith, to speak of God and to talk of their own lives in terms of an arena where God is present. For newcomers to faith this is a vital but often difficult transition.

2 Roger L. Walton, *The Reflective Disciple: Learning to Live as Faithful Followers of Jesus in the Twenty-first Century*, London: SCM Press, 2010; see esp. chapter 4: 'The Rhythm of Discipleship'.

They have grown up in a culture that has no such vocabulary. For longer-term members of the Church it is something of a lost art.[3] For both groups the dominant media portrayal is of God language being at best quirky and at worst dangerous. The temptation then is to leave God language in the liturgy and keep it well apart from the stuff of ordinary life.

Ironically, lack of God language does not mean people have no experience of God. The work of David Hay, Rebecca Nye and others has consistently shown, from empirical studies, that many if not most adults and children have experience of the transcendent, but in a culture that no longer offers a language to speak of these experiences they tend to hide them and leave them undisclosed. With interested and non-judgemental listeners, many who describe themselves as without religion are prepared to share these significant moments.[4]

In the past, especially for Protestant Christians, the way into making connections between the language of faith and everyday life would have been through knowledge of the Bible. Children from a very early age would have learned Bible stories and adults would have used biblical language to interpret and give direction to their lives. It is now widely accepted that biblical literacy is at an all-time low in both society and in the Church in the UK.[5] The sometimes tired and poorly attended Bible study groups found in churches across the country are the last witness to a once strong and vibrant spirituality that drew on the Bible for its vocabulary. Most people now hear the words of the Bible only when they are read in church.

---

3 Methodist Church, *Time to Talk of God*, London: TMPC, 2005.

4 David Hay and Rebecca Nye, *The Spirit of the Child*, rev. edn, London: Jessica Kingsley, 2006; David Hay, *Something There: The Biology of the Human Spirit*, London: Darton, Longman & Todd, 2006.

5 According to 2008 National Biblical Literacy Survey, over 75 per cent of the UK population own a Bible but only 18 per cent open it weekly and 7 per cent daily. The story of Jesus' cross and resurrection were widely known but the parables of Jesus and much of the Old Testament were unknown, and under 19 per cent had any knowledge of the Ten Commandments. See Peter Phillips, 'National Biblical Literacy Survey 2008', Durham: CODEC, St John's College, University of Durham, 2009.

It seems unlikely that the Bible study group will revive in its old form. Indeed, many of the new patterns of Christian small-group study deliberately avoid its format; rather, they incorporate engagement with the Bible within a broader structure with the intention of ensuring reflection on personal discipleship and missional outreach. The first challenge for Christian education is then to find contemporary ways of allowing people to transfer the language of faith encountered in worship into the sphere of their lives, to become the interpretative tool for understanding and living their lives.

Opportunities for reflection

Learning the language of faith is not an end in itself, nor is it under-taken to be good at trivial pursuit or pub quizzes – indeed, these are the last places it would be valuable nowadays – but rather to enable interpretation and reflection. If, as David Tracy has put it, 'to be human is to be a skilled interpreter', then the language of faith facilitates such interpretation. It offers the words and con-cepts to think and speak theologically. Christian education must, as we have argued, work at the acquisition of faith language and couple this with the provision of opportunities for reflection.

Reflection is fundamentally a form of thinking that allows human beings to consider experience and previous understand-ings afresh, play imaginatively with meaning, find connections and insights that make better sense of life and provide a more secure basis on which to make decisions.[6]

What disciples often lack is a space where reflection can happen. Here Christian education plays a vital role. In the busy, often hectic lives that people lead and in the midst of a Church that is increasingly outreach- and service-driven, the role of Christian education is to create spaces for reflection. These can be simple structures: asking people to pause at the end (or in the middle of) a church business meeting to consider how what they are doing

---

6 See Walton, *Reflective Disciple* and Jennifer A. Moon, *Reflection in Learn-ing and Professional Development: Theory and Practice*, Abingdon and New York: Routledge, 2000.

links to their faith or the work of the Church; encouraging people in a worship service to talk to their neighbour about something that has been troubling them (or exciting them) in the last week and asking this partner to pray a prayer – both the telling and the praying may help reflection; gathering together youth workers to share experience and the challenges of their current work and posing the question: Where have you seen God in your work recently?

This is classically where process is more important than content. The content in terms of the substance or experience is already there. The educational dynamic lies in the permission-giving to pause and the encouragement to reflect.

One of the most powerful programmes running in the Methodist Church is known locally as Encounter.[7] It is a year-long journey for a small number of folk – usually up to a dozen – who come together because they have a hunch they are at a change-point or crossroads in their lives. They have monthly meetings and various inputs are offered to stimulate thought, but the core question of the whole programme is: What does God want me to do? No one thinks this will be answered by an instant message on a wall – discernment is rarely that simple. What the course offers more than anything else is a series of meeting spaces where this can be the main question. It is a gathering of companions who are asking the same question, so there are opportunities for conversation, sharing of stories and a chance to see what faith-sense others are making. The structure also provides accompanists – folk with some experience of the same sort of journey – so each individual has a partner with whom to talk and check out their own inclinations and attempts at discernment. It is an example of an opportunity for reflection.

Another such reflection space is the growing practice of This Time Tomorrow or TTT slots in worship.[8] Often taking place in the mid-morning Sunday gathering, this is where individuals are

7 Encounter is the name given to the form of a programme known more generically as EDEV (Extending Discipleship, Exploring Vocation).

8 This idea is promoted by the London Institute for Contemporary Christianity (LICC).

invited to say what they will be doing this time tomorrow (say on Monday at 11 a.m.): what tasks they will tackle and what challenges they face as Christians in the workplace or at home the next day. This short reflection is often followed by prayer for the person or persons who have spoken and the people they will engage with.

My own research suggests that transferring reflection skills from one setting to another is not straightforward. People have to learn to begin again with another kind of focus. At different times it can be on personal life challenges, work dilemmas, understanding the theological themes in a 'secular' film or novel, the business before church council. Christian education has a pivotal part to play in this by engineering regular and varied opportunities for reflection.[9]

Providing core and critical skills

Core skills for living in the rhythm include language work, as outlined above, but also helping people learn to pray (taking the conversation with God in worship into personal life), exploring a basic Christian framework of belief such as those included in confirmation, membership or enquirers' courses and practising Christian lifestyle values such as putting others' needs first, forgiveness and care for the poor. All these are forms of scaffolding that enable the linking of the three spheres of formation. They need not be formalized as classes or courses. There is good evidence they can be effectively learned through mentoring, prayer triangles and small-group meetings, particularly if set up with these outcomes in mind.

I do want to make a plea, however, that critical skills be included at an early stage. There is a narrative that runs something like this:

I became a Christian through an evangelical church. Here I met Christians who had strong faith. Because of their witness I gave

9 Roger L. Walton, 'The Teaching and Learning of Theological Reflection: Case Studies of Practice', PhD thesis, University of Durham, 2002.

my life to Christ and began to study the Bible and pray. The Church's teaching was clear and straightforward and took the Bible at face value as being literally the true word of God. Later on through various experiences I began to be unsure of this form of literalism and was introduced to more critical ways of reading the Bible. This created doubts in my mind and something of a crisis of faith, but gradually I began to see that even if the virgin birth or a physical ascension were not factual but more metaphorical, and while some parts of Scripture contradict others, God's life-giving truth is still to be found in the Bible.

This not uncommon story is sometimes described as the journey to a second naivety – wherein critical thinking and hermeneutics of suspicion are known and valued but trust in God remains simple and real, and often stronger, as a result.

There are those who think this journey of faith – from pre-critical to critical to post-critical – is inevitable, and James Fowler's theory of stages of faith development seems to be borne out in this story and in the large numbers of young people drawn into conservative evangelical churches who later either lose faith or transfer to churches that embrace a broader range of theologies. My own view is that this is not an invariant sequence and that critical awareness and critical thinking can be built in at the early stages of engagement with the faith. We know this from other fields of education and even from popular culture. Take the deconstructing and reconstructing of fairy tales in films such as *Shrek*. Here there is a form of (adult) knowing in the repositioning of the 'ogre' as the hero and in the humorous anti-hero dialogue that ironically still promotes enduring virtues such as truth, love and loyalty. Interestingly this not only works for adults who 'knew the original fairy stories' but also for children who are encountering *Shrek* alongside the old stories. They learn very quickly to live with the knowledge that stories can be deconstructed and reconstructed just as they learn to relate to mobile phones before they are a year old! Technically this is called meta-cognition, and is possible when new understandings live alongside old ones in the culture.

Critical engagement is important for discipleship in order to relate the world and faith to each other. People need to have critical awareness about how faith systems are humanly constructed and how in wider society power play and spin operate on a daily basis, making issues of justice and truth more difficult to locate. Neither of these means there is no reality behind the human constructions. Critical realism is for everyone! Christian education has a degree of responsibility for helping people learn and use critical skills.

All these components are ways of working with the rhythm of gathering and dispersing and developing a more robust spirituality for the task of discipleship.

Task 2: Building the body

The second major task of Christian education is to build the body of Christ. We noted in our explorations of mission, worship and community as formational agents that being linked with others was an intrinsic part of the experience. We are formed by God as we interact with each other in the light of the kingdom. Difference and diversity play a vital part in this process by bringing disciples face to face with that which is 'other' and requiring that we not only respect and honour difference but also allow the interaction of difference to create something new in us and in the world.

The New Testament in different ways speaks of this deep connection to one another and interaction of individuals in a variety of metaphors, but the most prominent image is that of the body. In Paul's first letter to the Corinthians he writes 'For just as the body is one and has many members, and all the members of the body, though many, are one body, so it is with Christ' (1 Cor. 12.12). He goes on to address one of the issues that is a great difficulty for the Corinthians Christians, namely that some in the community feel their gifts are not as useful or valued as others'. Paul's response is to say that if the whole body were an eye there would be no hearing, and if an ear, how would the body sense the various smells around? His point is that the varied gifts make up the whole and its ability to function as the body of Christ.

His final section before turning to the supremacy of love is to say that the gifts of God expressed in different kinds of ministries are precisely to make the body function properly. In other words, difference and diversity work together for good in this organism.

The same theme is taken up in Ephesians 4. Here the inter-action of the various parts causes everything to work together, to build up love, so that all might attain full maturity in Christ (Eph. 4.15–16).

In terms of building up the body, Christian education needs to work on aspects of the gathering and dispersing community to nurture, support and maximize the call to embrace difference and to release the potential of diversity. Christian education can play its part in three areas.

Meeting

In the Epistle to the Hebrews there is an exhortation about 'not neglecting to meet together' (Heb. 10.25). Each time I read this I smile. Much of my life is taken up with meetings of various sorts, to the point where I sometimes think they are the very enemy of getting anything done! Of course, the context of the Epistle is very different from mine. In this small, persecuted first-century Christian Church the reasons to be tempted to give up meeting would have been the fear of discrimination and even violence. The kind of meeting the author has in mind here may well be the once-per-week meeting for worship and fellowship, where the different members of the community encountered each other and sought to come close to God. Beneath the notion of meeting as getting together is a deeper dynamic. In this gathered church community that brings together rich and poor, men and women, slave and free, children and adults, saints and sinners, there is encounter in a new way, where difference no longer dictates to people their place in the pecking order of society but affords discovery, insight, healing and complementarity. When Paul says 'There is no longer Jew or Greek, there is no longer slave or free, there is no longer male and female; for all of you are one in Christ Jesus' (Gal. 3.28), he does not mean that these are no longer part of our experience and identity but that in Christ all differences have new meaning and new potential. Later he speaks of difference as being caught up in a new creation (Gal. 6.15).

Real encounters create new understanding, empathy and insight. This often comes as a delightful surprise.

Inderjit Bhogal, the leader of the Corrymeela community in Northern Ireland, tells the story of wrestling with a sermon he was preparing on the text 'a table in the wilderness' (Ps. 78.19) as he took one of his regular walks in a park in central Sheffield and sat down alongside a homeless man he had spoken with several times before. He shared with the man the task before him – a talk on bread and parties and wilderness – and immediately the man started talking about bread:

'I love bread', he said.

He reached into a carrier bag beside him. His boots and walking stick were by the bag. Out of the bag he fetched bread. 'I always have bread', he said. 'I know a shop. I turn up just before closing time. They give me a couple of loaves. With it I feed myself and my brothers and sisters who are poor.' He talked to me about all those homeless ones who walk at night as others sleep.

He held out a large round cob.

'This is made from rye. I love it – my favourite.' He said, 'Try some.'

He broke off a large piece with his rugged hands and held it out to me. I received it and said 'Amen' and ate it in bits over several minutes.

As I ate it, he unpacked his carrier bag and brought out different kinds of bread and placed it all on the concrete slab bench, which had now become a table. Suddenly I was having a meal, and he was the host. Each loaf was held up and its contents were described. I was given a piece from each loaf.

'You need good red wine with this bread … it would be a good one for your communion at church.'

'You need to eat this bread with cheese …'

All around us a city-centre environment with its own beauty, but a wilderness with a lifestyle of grabbing and greed and of profit before people. People racing about. Some sitting down to rest. Before me now a parable of the text: 'a table in the wilderness'. I was being fed by one of the poorest people I know. I was a guest of honour at a table in the wilderness.[10]

The same kind of eye-opening revelation can happen when people of different sexualities meet and talk, when people of different faiths share at a deep and personal level, when victims come face to face with those responsible for the crimes that have hurt them.

Christian education can facilitate such meeting. Of course, it will begin with those already in the life of the Church – there is much difference to work with here – but must also extend encounter beyond to the wider sphere of God's realm, namely the whole of creation.

Welcoming

Recently we attended a church we had never visited before. We were met by a welcome steward. Her job was to spot and look after newcomers. She talked to us, introduced us to others, took us to the front of the coffee queue – as this was the church's policy for first-timers – and gave us a welcome pack before we left. It was a good experience, a far cry from those tales of folk going to church for the first time and being ignored; and yet it is only the surface meaning of the notion of hospitality in the New Testament.

There are two words in the New Testament for hospitality. One means 'love of strangers'. The use of this word echoes such texts as Deuteronomy 10.16–18, where God loves strangers and provides for them. The implication is: if God looks after strangers, so must God's people. This is the word used in Hebrews 13.2, where the writer says 'Do not neglect to show hospitality to strangers,

---

10 This story was shared at the Methodist Conference in 2000. The full sermon can be found at inderjitbhogal.com/wp-content/Atableinthewilderness.pdf.

for by doing that some have entertained angels without knowing it.' The other word means 'to make space for a guest'. It is used in Acts when Simon the tanner makes space for Peter to lodge in his home (Acts 10.6), but is also used when the Athenians hear Paul making his speech in the Areopagus. They wanted to hear – to make space for – the surprising new things Paul was proclaiming (Acts 17.20). They opened their ears to something strange and made a little room for this 'other'. Hospitality therefore might be defined as 'To make space at your table, in your life and in your heart for the stranger. To welcome and respect that which is strange and different, and to make room for it.'

It is more than a friendly welcome on your first visit to a church; rather, it is a way of being church that is always changing to accommodate and learn from the newcomer. The story of the family from the Congo, which I told in Chapter 2, captures this well (see p. 24). The friendliness of the church congregation was translated into adapting the life of the community to be larger and more inclusive, so making a new creation.

Building up the body of Christ involves establishing and developing a culture of hospitality, and this is an educational enterprise. It is educational in that it is counter-intuitive and needs to be learned. Our natural tendencies are to establish patterns and boundaries and welcome others only on our terms. God's kingdom seems to be different and the people of God are called to learn and adopt God's ways of hospitality. Jesus did, after all, suggest that when we have a party we should not invite those who will invite us in return; rather, the poor and vulnerable who cannot return the favour. Christian education can play a big part in providing opportunities to think about and practise the ways of hospitality.

Connecting

The third part of building the body is the business of connecting. The body of Christ is not just a local congregation, nor an associated group of churches, but the people who hear and respond to God's love across the world and across time. A church not connected with this wider Christian community is not a church at all. Learning about and from the church down the road and the church 10,000 miles away is a part of becoming the body of Christ. Such learning reminds us and reinforces for us that God loves the world (John 3.16), not just some in it or some parts of it. We all are held in God's loving intent.

Likewise learning about our connectedness to the Early Church, the church of the Reformation period and the churches of the poorest and wealthiest parts of the world in the twenty-first century in all their glory and all their failures is a recognition of who we are and what we are called towards.

There has been a shift in the ecumenical agenda in the UK in the last 40 years. We have moved away from recognizing one another, talking about our differences and striving to be one national church. Nowadays it is more common to find churches in a locality cooperating on street pastors, food banks and fresh expressions of church such as Messy Church. This local ecumenical mission agenda not only connects churches to each other in creative ways to do pieces of work they could not do on their own but also connects the churches to the needs of their immediate communities.

The role of Christian education should be obvious. Where Christian communities do not recognize their belonging together in God or are disconnected from the needs of the world, Christian education must create learning opportunities for understanding and connecting so that both mission and worship can be enriched and be located in the wider work of God. Christian education will also play a part in alerting and enabling such missional engagement to be a source of new learning. The recent involvement of churches in the provision of food for the hungry and destitute through food banks has led many to consider the sources of poverty in the modern world, the issues of tax justice, the importance of fair and open trade and the need to pay proper prices for goods or risk perpetuating the dangers of sweatshop labour in Bangladesh, for example. A group of churches in West Yorkshire involved in food distribution, debt counselling and provision for the homeless called together other caring agencies, faith communities, local councillors and national politicians to share what they were learning and explore what they should do. It was a work of Christian education, forming disciples and building up the body of Christ for more effective action.

Task 3: Extending and enhancing mission, worship and community

The third major task of Christian education is to be a resource for developing mission, worship and community. In this sense it is a critical friend to all three. It performs its task through three actions: enabling honest appraisal; drawing on the tradition; generating new knowledge. All of these can contribute to the ongoing growth and development of the life of mission, worship and community, and as these are the primary agents for the formation of disciples, Christian education will thus exert influence in the forming of disciples.

Enabling honest appraisal

It is always refreshing to have a new member of a team. They ask the questions others no longer ask: Why do we do this? Why do we always follow that pattern? What does that logo mean? What are we aiming at? It is not that those who have been there a longer time could not ask these questions or do not on some occasions, it is simply that they are so used to the way things are, it is difficult to think about them in a fresh way or imagine them in a radically different form. When stuck on a crossword clue, often I cannot see what my wife or friend sees as the answer not because I do not know the word but because in considering the clue I cannot shift from my initial way of thinking.

In worship, mission and community we get stuck. We become used to ways of thinking and acting and cannot envisage things operating in a different way. The role of Christian education here is to find ways of allowing us to see with new eyes or from a different vantage point. Take the example of children and Holy Communion. Not many years ago most UK Protestant churches would not allow children to share in bread and wine. Now, though some churches would reserve taking bread and wine to adults, a large number have moved to the position that children who are regular worshippers and have the consent of their parents are invited to receive the elements. When the idea was first mooted, most could not see how it could be. Children do not understand what communion is about said some; they should wait until they believe said others; and what if they do not take communion seriously and thus trivialize it? Advocates pointed out that none of us truly understands what communion is; that many children have a deep and profound belief and trust in God; and that when it had been tried, children sensed and responded to the significance of the occasion. One of the most telling arguments for me was when someone pointed out that the physical things to which children relate – food and drink – and which in most families are signs of belonging, were carrying the opposite message in the Church. By being excluded from these concrete signs of God's love, children were subtly being told that they did not yet belong fully. Once I had seen it from this angle I could appreciate that there was an agenda to examine wherein we could better express what it means to be part of a people worshipping God.

Enabling honest appraisal need not be a hyper-critical process. Seeing things from a new perspective may highlight good and valuable things that should not only be preserved but built on.

Drawing on the tradition

There is a role for Christian education in keeping people in touch with the traditions from which they come and the history within which they are located. This is not tradition with a small 't' that has often come to mean customs going back little further than recent memory. It is the deep-rooted sources of energy that gave birth to particular movements and churches and endowed them with life and passion. As Martyn Atkins argued, finding and revisiting the original charisms within a tradition can be a source of its renewal.[11]

---

11 Martyn Atkins, *Resourcing Renewal: Shaping Churches for the Emerging Future*, Peterborough: Epworth Press, 2010.

Terry Veling put it like this:

Tradition calls out to us from the deep memory of the past, not to celebrate nostalgia or comforting doctrines, not to enshrine some truth in a timeless vault. It is not quaint or comforting reminiscence; rather it is the memory of a passionate people with deeply spiritual longings and burning hearts. Tradition is the collective and living memory of a people, but what they remember is not a 'glorious past' to be revered and enshrined. Rather they remember a time that has not yet arrived. Paradoxically, they carry and preserve the memory of a future that is yet to be, a time that is still coming, a promise that still beckons and asks us to respond.[12]

By offering study and storytelling, primary sources and pilgrimages, Christian education can put communities in touch with their own tradition and the traditions of the wider Christian community, which in turn can encourage confidence and inspire new ventures in mission and worship for the kingdom. The emerging church and fresh expressions movements often use the slogan 'Ancient-Future', meaning that they are looking to the deep and original traditions of the Church not to replicate them but to give inspiration and direction into God's future and the creating of the new.

Generating new knowledge

Finally, Christian education acts to help create new knowledge and embed the learning in the ongoing life of the Church. It creates new knowledge by helping people to reflect on their experience of mission, worship and community and share the stories of God that are new and vital. This comes in the form of personal testimony but also in creative acts of worship, formal statements, press releases, website videos, tweets and posters. Christian education has the role of gathering wisdom and insight and holding it to

---

12 Terry A. Veling, *Practical Theology: "On Earth as It Is in Heaven"*, Maryknoll, NY: Orbis Books, 2005, p. 37.

serve as a reminder and encouragement to Christian communities of what has been learned on the way and needs to shape its life, worship and mission. Even the humble flip chart with its scrawled writing that for a moment has captured gems of inspiration or moments of clarity is a vital part of this function.

One of the most interesting and imaginative initiatives of recent years has been the ARCS (Action Research Church and Society) project, based in London. This was a group of professional theologians, researchers and educators who offered their time and energy to churches and Christian agencies to help them understand and strengthen their work and witness. Together the groups identified an area to examine and agreed a research question. Having collected data, both the theologians and the church or agency staff reflected separately and then together, with a focus on the theological as well as practical learning there was to be distilled. Over four years ARCS worked with 12 different partners, including a parish church, a Christian housing association and a Catholic youth-work agency. In each case the research was able to uncover insights that strengthened mission, enhanced worship and provided new ways of thinking about the work.[13] This approach is at the heart of good Christian education in generating new knowledge.

Of course, these findings must avoid becoming the doctrines and traditionalism that stultifies the future but rather contribute wisdom to the living tradition and active mission of the Church. They can be recognized for the treasures they are and brought out with the old treasures to offer a rich trove of learning that aids and assists the forming of God's people in the image and likeness of God.

---

13 For a full account of the project and its methods, see Helen Cameron et al., *Talking About God in Practice: Theological Action Research and Practical Theology*, London: SCM Press, 2010.

The tasks of Christian education

To summarize, the work of Christian education can be set out as follows:

Working with the rhythm of discipleship:

- to help people learn and use the language of faith;
- to offer opportunities for reflection;
- to develop core and critical skills.

Building the body:

- to enable meeting;
- to nurture hospitality;
- to connect the church.

Extending and enhancing mission, worship and community:

- to enable honest appraisal;
- to draw on the tradition;
- to generate new knowledge.

In this chapter we have outlined a calling and agenda for Christian education in the forming of disciples. It is a derived and secondary force relying on the engagement of individuals and communities with worship, mission and community. In relation to this ongoing immersion of followers in the gathered and dispersed Church, Christian education has a vital part to play, with God's grace, to form disciples.

Reflections and Questions on Section 1

If I am right in the argument through Chapters 1 to 4, namely that the primary agents for forming disciples are mission, worship and community, and that Christian education plays a supporting role, there are a number of issues about our current discourses and practices on the subject of discipleship that might benefit from further thought. I pose here some brief questions and reflections you might like to consider.

Enquirers' courses

Enquirers' courses such as Alpha, Start! and Emmaus are structured to help people understand Christian belief and then decide whether they want to consider it further, sign up or walk away. Initiators of these courses and short programmes have worked hard at enabling enquirers to feel at ease in non-threatening settings with meals, videos and small-group activities, but the main content is Christian beliefs. One should not underestimate the power of personal testimony in this context, given by Christians who lead or speak or share in groups, but it remains true that the emphasis is mostly on Christian beliefs. Broadly, the courses say: 'This is what Christians believe. Do you want to take it further?' I question how well this approach works with the formational energies identified in this section. In the Early Church the catechumenate experience included lifestyle changes (such as giving up violence, false trading and drunkenness), engagement in mission (such as visiting the poor) and attendance at worship (at least up until the sermon). Catechumens – the Early Church's enquirers

– were learning what faith is by participation, alongside being presented with the Christian world view.[1]

Mark Scandrette argues provocatively that engagement in Christian practices should be the main vehicle for discovering the transformative power of Jesus. It is by 'experimenting' with the core practices advocated by Jesus – giving to the poor, working with the marginalized, living simply and trusting God's benevolence – that one enters into the truth, healing and hope of the gospel. He calls for the use of a Jesus dojo rather than a classroom or discussion group. A dojo is a practice space often associated with martial arts but the term could be applied to any space used for practical skill development (such as a cooking dojo).[2] His point is that we need to move to active participation in the kingdom as a way of knowing it.

I wonder whether we might include more by way of experiencing practices in our enquirers' courses as well as encouraging a trial period in worship. The practice might be going out with street pastors, working at the homeless shelter or hospital visiting, preferably with a mentor and conversation partner so there can be reflection on the experience and so that this could feed into any meeting for the discussion of faith. This could be harder to invite people into but might set the enquiry into the primary formative framework from the beginning of the journey, so that people do not get the idea faith is first belief, then worship and finally mission.

Sharing divine discoveries

When I talk to groups about these ideas on formation the response is generally positive. They like the idea of the rhythm of gathering and dispersing as God's people, and folk agree that we are

---

1 There is a short, useful summary of Cyprian as a Catechumen in Liz West and Trevor Withers, *Walking Together: Making 21st Century Disciples*, Harpenden: Cell UK Ministries, 2011, pp. 14–15.

2 Mark Scandrette, *Practicing the Way of Jesus: Life Together in the Kingdom of Love*, Downers Grove, IL: InterVarsity Press, 2011.

formed as we meet God in worship and in the life of the world. The notion that God is in the midst of life and speaking to us within it – as well as in the worship event – is attractive, but when I ask about the opportunities in their gathered church for sharing of our divine discoveries made in the world, there is something of a quiet wondering. Some say this happens in their small-group meetings, others that it is more a matter of one-to-one sharing. There are rarely any examples of such sharing opportunities connected with congregational worship. It seems this time is primarily for reminding ourselves of the mighty acts and character of God as revealed in Jesus and the Bible, and if it is related to our everyday lives it is primarily an application of principles and insights to be able to live better. This is, of course, an important part of the reason for meeting together, but if we believe that God is active in the world and our everyday lives, there must be much to be gained from sharing our experience of God when we gather.

As we shall see later, small groups can provide this kind of space, but I wonder whether there is something symbolic as well as essential in creating structures and spaces for such conversation and reflection in the worshipping community. I am struck by the seamless transition from report into worship in the story of Acts 4. Here Peter and John tell of their experience and immediately the community is caught up in prayer and praise (Acts 4.23). What kinds of structure could make such sharing regular and normal at gatherings for worship?

Ministerial training

It should be clear that the preparation and development of those called to leadership and ordained ministries in the life of the Church has to include continued engagement in mission, worship and community, whatever else it may contain. Ministers remain disciples and disciples go on being formed. There are questions, however, about the self-perception of training institutions. In reality they are often hybrid establishments, in part shaped by the academic forms of higher education and subject to the scrutiny of university inspectorates, and in part created to educate and evaluate people in whom churches can put their trust for public leadership and ministerial competence. Some institutions will see themselves leaning more towards the former and some very strongly towards the latter. Most will have a diet of worship and learning in community.

I wonder how the sense of identity as a missionary community can best be expressed in training for ministers. I do not mean, in saying this, that I think training institutions omit this from their life. I have not yet encountered training for ministry in college, course or scheme, part-time, full-time or church-based, that did not have mission and worship in its life and in all probability at the heart of its mission statement. Rather, I mean: How can this identity be perceived by all involved in its life, from new student to caretaker and principal?

Andrew Wingate argues quite forcibly that ministerial training structures can easily be a way of holding mission at arm's length; that its worship and community life can become divorced from the sharp end of mission and so risk superficiality. The monastic structure that has been dominant for 200 years in seminaries majors on community and worship and makes forays into mission, for learning and reflection. He compares this with the mission projects that grew from and were sustained in his previous training institution in Tamilnadu, India – work among prisoners, prostitutes and orphans. These were not initiatives of local churches that students visited but an essential part of the work of the seminary, which started and developed them. They embodied the idea that the theological institution is itself an initiator of mission, and as such, mission is central to its life. As a result Wingate advocates choosing locations and missional enterprises that strengthen this identity in the UK. The question underlying his suggestion is worth pondering.[3]

All these examples highlight to a greater or lesser extent some imbalance in the engagement with the primary formational

---

3 Andrew Wingate, *Does Theological Education Make a Difference? Global Lessons in Mission and Ministry from India and Britain*, Geneva: WCC Publications, 1999.

energies, in particular the tendency to see mission as an outworking of Christian faith rather than formative of discipleship. We will encounter this in the second half of the book also, as we consider small groups.

Section 2

Small Groups and Discipleship Formation

The first section of the book set out a view of discipleship formation. It is as people worship God, live as an intentional Christian community and seek to be engaged in the *missio Dei* that Christian disciples are formed. Christian education is the term we have given to the work of the Church in supporting and strengthening this formational process. It works with the rhythm of mission and worship, builds up the body and feeds back into mission, worship and community so that the Church can be faithful and the members can be formed in the ways of God.

In recent times the role of small groups in discipleship formation has been given much attention, and they are widely promoted as the key means for such formation. As one person puts it: 'We are about discipleship, and we believe that it happens best in small groups.'[1] Small-group membership is strongly encouraged now in many of the major denominations and is an almost essential feature of many of the new churches,[2] so much so that Helen Cameron identifies the small-group church as a new form of Church.[3]

As a form of Christian education, small groups have much to commend them. In this section we will explore them from a variety

---

1 Jim Putnam, *Real-Life Discipleship: Building Churches that Make Disciples*, Colorado Springs, CO: NavPress, 2010.

2 The Methodist Church and the Church of England both have promoted and begun to collect statistics on small groups.

3 Helen Cameron, *Resourcing Mission: Practical Theology for Changing Churches*, London: SCM Press, 2010, pp. 24–37.

of angles. In Chapter 5 there is an outline of what is meant by small groups and how they have been used in different contexts. The information is deliberately drawn from sources both within and beyond the Church's life, so that we are reminded that small groups are not exclusive to the Church and to provide a critical base with which to engage our church-based experience. Chapter 6 gives a brief history and analysis of the form of small groups in the churches over the twentieth century, while Chapter 7 provides an overview of recent research work on Christian small groups. In Chapter 8 we offer an outline process for developing the use of small groups in a church setting.

Although I have some passion for small-group work in church and think there are ways to achieve good outcomes, including the task of helping to form disciples, there is an implicit recognition throughout that it is not the only way to undertake discipleship formation. Christian education is bigger than what happens in and through small groups. Much of our thinking and planning needs to be about what is done through small groups and what must be done via other means. The final chapter is thus a theological reflection on the nature of forming disciples together and a challenge to the Church for this ministry.

5

The Value of Small Groups

You cannot read any of the Gospel accounts of the life of Jesus without noticing that he spent a lot of time with 12 people. In modern sociological terms this would be classified as a small group.

Small groups have a track record in Christian history, to which we will return later in the book. In the last 100 years, however, they have been a focus of attention for many people in education and business and have been subjected to much research by sociologists, psychologists and anthropologists. In this chapter we will look at the notion of a small group, explore the uses of small groups in contemporary society and discuss the ways small groups may be valuable for the formation of Christian disciples.

What is a small group?

Small group is a term that can be used in many ways. A collection of people waiting at a bus stop or on a station platform may be described as a 'small group of passengers', but although the term is quite appropriate, we are aware that there are differences between this small group and some others. Take a small group of pensioners who meet each week to have tea, chat and play bridge, or a group of teenagers who gather at a swimming club on a Tuesday evening to practise and then sit around in the coffee area afterwards to talk about the next race event, as well as music, films, school, relationships and sport. There is a level of knowledge, friendship and engagement between the members of the second two groups that is not obviously present in the passenger queue.

In the early days of studying groups, researchers tended to try to identify the factors that would define the boundaries of what was meant by a small group. So on the issue of size, for example, the view is often taken that a small group is one with fewer than 25 members. This seems to be the upper size limit most people use to define whether or not they belong to a small group and has some basis in research. In the 1920s Frederic Thrasher studied adolescent gangs (here a neutral term for associations of young people). He noted that gangs tended to break up upon reaching a membership of 25, two or more gangs then forming in place of one. However, the crucial factor was not size itself but size related to communication. He found that maintaining the gang was dependent on whether what was said by one member could be heard by all. Once this was no longer possible the gang would break into smaller units or develop another structure, with an inner circle and a larger wider membership making up a club.[1]

Another boundary factor is the amount and level of contact between members. Clearly those waiting at a bus stop may talk to each other but unless they are regularly at the same stop at the same time or know each other from other contexts, the conversation is likely to be experienced as little more than passing the time of day. The small group as a distinct social form was thus seen as people in conversation with each other regularly and in such a way as to render the quality of the exchange deeper and more significant. Theodore Mills defined small groups as follows: 'units composed of two or more persons who come into contact for a purpose and who consider the contact meaningful'.[2]

---

1 Individuals surveyed by Robert Wuthnow who said they belonged to small groups were in groups of 25 or fewer. These self-defined levels are consistent with other research. In gangs studied by Thrasher over 70 per cent were in groups of 25 or fewer, with 44 per cent in groups of 5 to 15 members. See Robert Wuthnow, *Sharing the Journey: Support Groups and America's New Quest for Community*, New York and London: Free Press, 1996; Thrasher's research is cited in A. Paul Hare, *The Handbook of Small Group Research*, New York: Free Press, 1962, p. 226.

2 Theodore M. Mills, *The Sociology of Small Groups*, 2nd edn, Prentice-Hall Foundations of Modern Sociology Series, Englewood Cliffs and London: Prentice-Hall, 1984, p. 2.

Notice that Mills does not define the upper size limit of a small group; rather, he concentrates on the 'meaningful' contact and shared purpose. By meaningful he has in mind that each person participating considers the quality and significance of exchange between group members valuable to them. This then has an effect on size. What is the optimum size needed to maintain a good quality of relationship and good interaction? Researchers have noted that the number of relationships in a group grows rapidly as each new member is added. So in a group of 3 there are 3 symmetrical relationships, with 6 there are 15, with 10 there are 45 and with 15 members the number of relationships rises to 105.[3] Attention to all the members in a group will be very demanding as the number increases, and members tend be less satisfied with the experience.

Of course, this is turn may be influenced by the task and physical context. Some tasks are hindered by a group of only five members, needing a wider range of skills or experience; other group tasks can be achieved well by five members and would become less effective if more members were brought in. Some groups, such as an exercise class, can work with 20 or more and still allow for the kind of interaction members find satisfactory. Much depends on the nature of the task. Likewise, if the meeting space is modest or configured in such a way as to inhibit communication, adding extra members will complicate the process and make it more frustrating.

This early research tended towards definitions of small group that tried to identify all the factors to define a distinct phenomenon. When you take these points together you end up with a statement like this:

A small group is an intentional association of between 2 and 25 people over time for a shared purpose, where meaningful interaction is expected in fulfilling the group's task.

---

3 The number of relationships is calculated by the formula $x = (n^2 - n)/2$ where n is the number of members. See Hare, *Handbook of Small Group Research*, p. 228.

In recent thinking there has been more emphasis on the continuity between what we might call natural and created or artificial groups. Natural groups are those that form naturally without planning or design in the flow of society's life. You could say family, work colleagues and near neighbours – and even the bus queue – are natural groups in this way. Artificial groups are intentionally designed or developed for some reason. Any group – natural or artificial – may be strong or weak in terms of the amount of time spent together and quality of interaction between the members; it may be large or small in number; it may be orientated towards a certain age, gender or life experience. Tom Douglas identifies 11 criteria by which groups may be classified (see Table 1).

Table 1: Outlining the factors influencing small groups[4]

Criteria	Classification
Nature	Is this a natural or artificial group?
Origin	Was it created deliberately or spontaneously?
Leader	Is the leader's style directive or non-directive?
Location	In what environment does it meet (physical space; ethos and organizational structure)?
Members	How are members selected?
Outcome	What is the group's purpose?
Number	Is the group large (20 plus); medium (10 to 20) or small (under 10)?
Throughput	Will the membership remain the same or change? Is it open or closed to newcomers?
Orientation	What theoretical approach underlies the group (e.g. of the leader or sponsoring organization)?
Programme	What activities will the group engage in (e.g. talks, drama, discussion)?
Duration	How long will the meetings be and how long will the group exist?

4 Tom Douglas, *Survival in Groups: The Basics of Group Membership*, Buckingham: Open University Press, 1995.

Understanding any particular small group will depend on where on the spectrum between various poles the group can be identified. For example, the pensioners' bridge club is small (it has between six and ten members); it is artificial as it was created by a couple of friends who wanted to play bridge; its purpose is social contact and a shared hobby; it may be composed of one gender; the conversations, though friendly, do not usually involve deeply personal sharing of problems. There is, however, some sense of care for one another that has developed over time, and there would be greetings cards and telephone calls if one person were not able to attend a session through illness.

The kinds of group we have in mind in this chapter could be described in terms of being created (artificial) and small; that is, they have been intentionally brought into being to function with numbers often well under 25; where members have regular contact with each other; where there is some sense of shared purpose.

The uses of small groups

There are several established uses of small groups.

Care and support

Belonging to a group where you are known, valued and accepted is a source of great strength. It gives you a sense of identity and a set of people you can turn to when you face problems. Families are for many people such a support group. In most families individuals are loved and accepted as they are, and when difficulties present themselves, family members are usually ready with encouragement, comfort and practical help. Small groups can function for people like a family. As people get to know each other over time and build up an atmosphere of trust, they relax with each other and are prepared to reveal more about themselves. Relationships built in a small group are often extended through other contacts – telephone calls, meeting for coffee, sharing meals or simply bumping into each other in the street or supermarket – and friendships form. As result, folk are often more prepared to offer the support to one another the way families might.

This kind of belonging can grow in a group, even though its principal reason for meeting is not mutual support. Judith moved to a new area and job, but apart from her husband did not know anyone. Gradually she talked to neighbours and got to know a few of her work colleagues, but her sense of being 'more at home' changed when she joined a book club. It was advertised on the noticeboard of the library, indicating some of the novels the members were reading and giving a phone number. She rang up, got the details of meeting times and dates and went along. At the first meeting she was nervous and unsure whether her opinions would appear shallow in the discussion, but folk were very friendly and seemed genuinely interested in her and her views. Within six sessions of the fortnightly meetings she felt at home with the new contacts and enjoyed their humour. Reading and discussing the books were experiences she looked forward to, and it was fun simply being with this group. She met up with a couple of members on other occasions and began to share more deeply not only her own thoughts and views on the books but much about her life, work and even problems.

With the breakdown of more extended family networks due to increased mobility and the movement away from family homes of grown up children for study and work, there is evidence that people look to other groups to supply their sense of belonging and to gain support.

Even when they are close at hand, some families are or become dysfunctional and cannot offer the sense of support that we need. What is more, there are some experiences that may go beyond the resources of family networks. Take for example a family where a child is diagnosed with a relatively rare disease or meets a disaster that few others have encountered. When this kind of challenge confronts a person or nuclear family, they will often link with others whom they previously have not known but who can together share the pain and find ways of coping.

The following story, found on the Compassionate Friends web-site, is perhaps typical of the origins of many caring charities.[5]

The family was engaged in the usual early morning hassle as we washed, dressed, ate and finally shared a moment as the children left for school. We were four – Iris and Joe, parents, Angela (the elder of our children, aged nearly fifteen) and Kenneth – the younger, nearly twelve. The youngsters departed and then, minutes later, as we prepared to leave too, the telephone rang. I picked it up, a voice said, 'There's been an accident. Kenneth has been taken to hospital by ambulance.' We rushed to the hospital convincing each other that it could be nothing worse than a broken limb, but within a short time we knew that it was serious, he was unconscious; later we were told that he had suffered major head injuries, with resultant brain damage. We were face-to-face with death.

Elsewhere in the hospital was another boy, Billy Henderson, suffering from cancer. His parents had nursed him through a long illness, at his bedside day and night. We discovered later that the Henderson family (Bill and Joan, the parents, Andrew and Billy, their sons, and daughters, Shone and Susan) and ourselves were all known to the Rev. David Dale, a minister in the United Reformed Church.

Standing back from the constant group of relatives and friends round Kenneth's bed in the Intensive Care Unit was another young man in clerical garb, the Rev. Simon Stephens. He simply said, 'If I can help ... I am here, all of the time.' Eventually we asked, 'Will you pray for Kenneth', and when he did so, he mentioned Billy Henderson. Thus we came to know somewhere in this vast hospital another boy lay dying, another family hoped and prayed.

It was not to be. Kenneth died on 23rd May 1968 – a day now indelibly stamped in our memory. Billy Henderson died a few days later.

---

5 www.tcf.org.uk/.

Iris suggested that we send flowers to Joan and Bill; we did not then know the significance of that act, but looking back, it might be said that The Compassionate Friends started there. Joan and Bill telephoned their thanks and we met for a cup of tea. Together, midst freely-flowing tears, the four of us were able for the first time to speak openly of our children, without feelings of guilt that we were endlessly repeating the virtues of our children, and of our vanished hopes for the future. Together, we were all able to accept, for the first time, the words used by many well-meaning friends – rejected almost universally by parents who have lost a beloved child – 'I understand.' We did understand, all four of us, and, in the immensity of our grief (and in reality is there any other tragedy of quite this enormity?), we all suffered together.[6]

This was a traumatic event for four parents that resulted in a small group forming for mutual support in their grief. It was also the beginning of a charity that seeks to help others facing the tragic loss of a child. It is one example of many. The number of support groups or agencies in the UK alone is huge – a recent listing carried over 100 for problems beginning with the letter 'A' alone – and many of them tell similar stories of their genesis.

Small groups, then, often fill a gap and help to meet the needs experienced by particular people. They frequently work by putting folk in touch with others in the same situation and forming small support groups. Tom Douglas records the following story and reflection:

A group of single parents was formed by social workers after a great deal of hard work, which involved providing transport, a meal at each attendance and child-minding facilities. Initially, the members of the group were suspicious of each other, but as it became clear that they faced the same difficulties, they became freer in their conversation. The social workers, who were not new to groupwork, were surprised by the number of

6 Joe Lawley, 'The history of The Compassionate Friends', www.tcf.org.uk/?s=kenneth.

such statements as: 'Oh! I felt I was the only one who felt like that', or 'I am glad to hear that's what you do – I thought I was going barmy!'

When you know that others are acting, thinking and feeling about a problem which they have in common in roughly similar ways, because you can see and hear it happening, there is a powerful sense of relief which flows from that knowledge. It is even more powerful if the knowledge of similarity is acquired in a face-to-face situation, when it has the impact of direct personal understanding without the intervention of others. The individual's own senses have a higher degree of credibility than when information is conveyed by others.[7]

Coping with similar problems and challenges, these single mums found in their group a common bond, practical advice and ultimately a few supportive friends. This links to another related use of small groups, namely therapy. In the early years of the twentieth century Joseph Pratt used small groups for patients suffering from the same medical condition, beginning with sufferers from tuberculosis. He and others reported regularly that for patients 'the sociability engendered in the group is a therapeutic benefit'.[8] Since then it has been widely adopted as a usage of small groups. The approach was employed by Alcoholics Anonymous, which works on the principle that a small group can help motivate, maintain and support recovery.

Some small groups are set up for the purpose of mutual care and support. Others are not specifically formed for this purpose but find that one of the consequences of being together is that members give and receive care and that this is positively life enhancing. There are no guarantees on this front. Some small groups excel at pastoral care and some, like some families, fail to deliver for a variety of reasons. Nevertheless it is well established that small groups can be sources of care and support.

---

7 Douglas, *Survival in Groups*, p. 26.

8 J. H. Pratt, 'The Principles of Class Treatment and Their Application to Various Chronic Diseases', *Hospital Social Services* 6:6 (1922), pp. 401–17.

Learning

For most of the twentieth century small groups have been employed for learning. This has been true at almost every level and for most age groups. The reasons are not hard to see. In a small group tackling a learning task together or discussing a topic, a number of things can happen:

- You can pool information.
- You can express a view or opinion.
- You can gain insights that others have developed and you have not yet seen.
- You can share a problem and get a variety of ideas on how to solve it.
- You can draw on the differing abilities in the group.
- You can learn new ways of thinking and reasoning from others.

All this helps in constructing your own ideas, views and making your own meaning. One of the main theories of how we learn is that each of us builds our own knowledge base through a process of dialogue between new information or experience and what we know already. This process of making sense and making meaning is helped by having to express our ideas either orally or in writing and having to test them against the ideas – and challenges – of others. Hence group members discussing a book chapter, Bible passage or an issue such as abortion echo in their comments, assertions and disagreements the kind of internal conversation individuals have on the subject, but add to them by offering a wider range of perspectives and resources from each others' experience.

But we do not just assimilate or modify ideas in small groups. There is much more going on as we relate to others in the group. Perhaps the majority of our learning will be social and emotional rather than intellectual as we interact with others. You can see this most acutely in newcomers. If we are newcomers to a group, like Judith joining her book club, we are joining an established community. It will have an existing pattern for the meeting and some ground rules about how people speak and act in the group (even if these do not exist in any formal way or the members of the group could not tell you them beforehand). As we participate in a group we are absorbing the patterns of behaviour as well as the group norms, values and emotions. In the early stages most newcomers are alert to the types of behaviour members exhibit and notice what is acceptable and unacceptable in the group. They will usually adjust their behaviour so they too can fit in and belong in the group. Over the longer term, once newcomers begin to feel comfortable relating in the group they will gradually become aware of and engage with the values and goals that drive its life. Again this may not be all at a conscious level and may involve some implicit and accidental testing of what seems important. The person who says in a group, 'I know you will probably disagree with this but ...' may well be checking out the values the group holds rather than simply starting a discussion. In time people gradually learn what the group feels strongly about, what you can make fun of and how to express emotions in the group. This social learning goes on well beyond the newcomer stage of course. It continues throughout the group's life but members over time become sensitized and know how to relate to the group's emotions, values and norms.

Thus learning in groups is never just about ideas or views. In any situation our learning is related to our social relations and the cultures or subcultures that inform the context. Sometimes people use the word socialization to describe the effect groups can have on newcomers. As the group's style and pattern are expressed in the interaction between members, newcomers learn how to participate more fully by adopting these practices themselves. This need not be seen as a negative process, neither is it one-way. Most people want to fit into the new situations and most small groups adapt a little as new people join. Because of this small groups can be also very helpful for integrating people into larger structures or communities. Research on personnel joining large companies found that small workgroups were central to whether they felt part of the organization. In fact the workgroups were more important than training or induction programmes. If colleagues in their small workgroup felt positive about the company and were committed to its values, and if the group helped new employees filter information to meet their needs, then the newcomers quickly integrated and felt positive about their job and the company.[9]

The point is that learning in a small-group setting is more than the facts or ideas that people absorb or develop. Members learn how to be in this setting as they notice and often adopt the attitudes and values that the group holds. They may imitate practices they value, both in the group and when outside it. Indeed it is sometimes obvious from members' mannerisms use that they have – often subconsciously – assumed the gestures and body language of others in the group. Just as we grow up unconsciously learning the accents of our parents and our school friends, so a strong small group shapes us in a whole range of ways often without our noticing.

Thus a small group can be a place for learning and change, even if the main purpose of coming together regularly is not specifically to learn. Where there is a learning agenda, such as knowing more about how your car works, how to do quilting or what is in the Bible, the group – its leaders or teacher – will employ particular methods that enable the specific knowledge and skills needed to grow, but in addition members will be learning as much from participating as from the subject matter.

Achieving a shared task

People working together can often accomplish much more than individuals on their own and sometimes more than they expect as a collection of people. The year 2007 marked the 200th anniversary of the Slave Trade Act, which banned slave trading in the British Empire, while 2006 had seen the release of the film *Amazing Grace*. Thus many people have become aware that William Wilberforce was not the sole hero of this story; rather, he worked

---

9 Richard Moreland and John Levine, 'Socialization in Organizations and Work Groups', in John M. Levine and Richard L. Moreland (eds), *Small Groups: Key Readings*, Key Readings in Social Psychology, New York and Hove: Psychology Press, 2006, pp. 469–98.

together with others for such an outcome. In particular he was a member of the Clapham Sect, a Christian group who met to campaign for social changes in the arenas of child labour, debt and the slave trade. In the face of massive vested interests, much of their success was due to working as a small group. They would have recognized that 'there are many things that human beings wish to do that can be accomplished by several people acting in concert'.[10]

Working as a small group can utilize many features that are essential for achieving a task:

- clarifying the task and the strategies or steps to achieve it;
- encouraging and motivating each other for the task;
- using a range of different members' skills;
- subdividing the work for more effective and efficient working;
- drawing on the wider resources and networks of individual members;
- holding members accountable for their part.

It is perhaps not surprising that ever since Elton Mayo found that industrial output was significantly affected by the network of group relations among workers, researchers have been interested in what makes some small groups or teams effective in achieving their goals and others less so.[11] Perhaps the most well-known studies are those carried out by Meredith Belbin at the Henley Management College in the 1970s. Belbin imagined that teams composed of highly intelligent people would succeed best, but this often proved false in experiments as in real life. In fact he concluded from his studies that the most successful teams or companies were those with a mixture of different 'types' of people working closely together. These include such types as 'a coordinator' – someone who helps everyone focus on their task; 'a plant' – someone who can solve difficult problems with original and creative ideas; 'a finisher' – someone who can reliably see things through to the end, ironing out the wrinkles and ensuring everything works well. Altogether he identified eight distinct types that

10 Douglas, *Survival in Groups*, p. 20.
11 See Mills, *Sociology of Small Groups*, p. 4.

make for a successful task-focused team. His classification was later changed to nine types and a psychometric test was developed for individuals to identify their types so that existing teams could assess their particular profile strengths and perhaps spot who or what their team needed to be more effective. Scholars have been divided about whether Belbin's types really stand up to analysis in all situations, but we do not have to subscribe fully to the theory to recognize that a combination of different personalities, skills and experience is likely to help the group be effective in pursuing its goals. The Belbin test remains a useful tool for groups to reflect on members' individual contributions and develop their working together. From our point of view, the very desire to attend to what makes for effective task groups shows the ability of small groups to tackle and often achieve concrete goals.

At the level of ordinary experience most of us have a positive experience of belonging to a small group that helped us achieve a goal we could not have achieved on our own. In my case I could cite planning a fundraising day, running a kids' holiday club and participating in team-sport competition.

Such small groups or teams are well placed for nurturing gifts and developing leadership. If there is sufficient trust and mutual support, and perhaps a strong sense of commitment to shared goals, small groups can provide a secure environment for individuals to try out new roles or take on new responsibilities, often surprising themselves with their new-found ability. In addition, members can model themselves on and be mentored by more experienced members of the group and its leaders. Many organizations intentionally structure their small groups to nurture individual skill as well as optimize task effectiveness.

Sustaining (alternative) values and commitments

Because small groups stand in an interesting relationship between individuals and much larger institutions and bodies, including society as a whole, they can function as places of resistance, often able to sustain a set of values and views in the face of a hostile culture. I can remember visiting Christian communities in East

Germany in the 1980s, before the fall of the Berlin Wall, who were not officially allowed to evangelize or engage in Christian education. The way they survived was through regular meetings in small groups, helping new Christians to learn and helping each other hold on to a world view that was at odds with the state and as a consequence might land them in jail or get them demoted at work. Base Christian communities in Latin America offer another example but there are many other non-Christian groups – including some who have been pressurized or persecuted by the Church – who have discovered the value of small groups for retaining an alternative world view in the face of an unsympathetic or even aggressive power. Indeed small groups have sometimes been the means of subverting the dominant discourse. Many innovative thinkers, artists, writers and scientists have managed to sustain their commitment to pioneering new developments against considerable opposition by belonging to small groups of those with similar desires, and others who have wanted to retain something they feared society would lose have been enabled to hold their ground because of the strength they drew from a supportive group.

This ability to provide a place of resistance and an alternative view of the world is another aspect of the socialization process of small groups we mentioned above. While the direction of socializing of some groups is conformity to the dominant values and views of the large body within which they exist, in other small groups members are able to assist each other in maintaining a radically different vision of reality and translating that into the way they live and engage with others.

Christian small groups

The four uses of groups identified under the four subheadings above are widely acknowledged. Of course, they are not mutually exclusive. You do not simply choose one of the four. There are almost always elements of each in any small group, and the study of how they relate to each other in particular groups or settings continues to be a major interest of psychologists and sociologists.

Small groups and their uses are also of interest to the churches. Because they are able to provide pastoral support and care, enable learning, achieve tasks, develop new skills and abilities, hold individuals accountable and support those under threat or desirous of making change, they are attractive to churches. Small groups are clearly tools capable of assisting the Church in its calling. No wonder, then, that they are a recurring feature of the Church's life through history. From the small house churches of the New Testament, through monastic orders, Puritan extended-family gatherings and Methodist class meetings to the cells of recent years, small groups have provided a means of enabling the Church to do its work and sometimes renew its sense of vocation.

In the first section of this book I outlined a view of discipleship formation as being enacted primarily through participation in mission, worship and community. Alongside these elementary forces I suggested that Christian education works with these primary agents in a variety of ways:

- to support Christians in moving between worship and mission, by developing the use of faith language, creating space for reflection and nurturing core and critical skills;
- to build the body of Christ by meeting, welcoming, connecting;
- to extend and enhance worship and mission via honest appraisal, exploring the tradition and generating new knowledge.

Much of this work could be undertaken and effectively accomplished in small groups. Their proven uses in a range of areas map well on to the agenda of Christian education. How small groups may be a part of Christian education will be explored in the next few chapters, beginning with an overview of the use of small groups in the life of the Church over the last century.

6

Small Group Explosion: Church Small Groups in the Twentieth Century

1900–40: study groups

Towards the end of the First World War the British government formed a working committee to draw up a plan for adult education to be implemented after the war. This work resulted in a report published in 1919 and thus is commonly known as the 1919 Report.[1] The report incorporated a survey of the educational work of many institutions in society and included a section on education provided by or through the churches. Here are some brief extracts from the report:

> In connection with the Society of Friends, a Central Study Committee has been set up, and under its auspices 35 study groups, comprising 520 students, have been formed. One of the keenest groups is comprised entirely of miners.
>
> A Diocesan Committee of the Diocese of Southwark came to the conclusion that there was 'a desire for a fuller and more exact knowledge of religious subjects which demanded and justified the setting up of the necessary new machinery'. The idea in mind was that a system of classes for the intensive study of theology, Christian Ethics, and other religious subjects

---

1 *The 1919 Report: The Final and Interim Reports of the Adult Education Committee of the Ministry of Reconstruction 1918-19*, Nottingham: Department of Adult Education, University of Nottingham, 1980.

should be instituted ... The basis of the classes is democratic; each class chooses its subject, and full and free discussion is a feature of the class meeting.

The Student Christian Movement has been responsible for some years past for a considerable number of classes and study circles concerned with Bible study, missionary work and social subjects ... The number of Bible Study Circles 2,411 – members 17,741.

There are similar accounts in the report of small-group-based study for the Wesleyans, the Roman Catholics, the Congregational Union, the Unitarians and various Christian movements and organizations within churches.

This snapshot of learning in the churches is valuable in two ways. First, it shows that small groups were alive and well in this period. The average number of those attending an SCM Bible-study group was seven. Groups of a similar size met as missionary-study circles and an average of eight people attended almost 1,000 social-study circles. Moreover the report acknowledges that what it presents by way of educational activities in the churches is primarily illustrative, detailed records not being available.[2] We know from other sources that there were many other small-group activities in the life of the churches. There were still, at this time, many Methodist class meetings. This group type had been inaugurated almost 175 years earlier by John Wesley, and although these declined in the nineteenth century they continued in many Methodist Churches well into the twentieth. Likewise small-group prayer meetings that were key mid-week and Sunday activities for many free churches are not referred to in the 1919 Report. Moreover, while the SCM Bible-study groups are mentioned, there is little reference to other Bible-study groups that were attached to a large number of Protestant churches. Small groups were clearly a feature of the life of many churches at the beginning of the twentieth century.

Second, the report indicates that many small groups in the life of the churches were for education. The educational endeavour

2 *The 1919 Report*, p. 251.

of these groups drew the notice of the compilers of the report. These, together with the summer schools, book production and lecture series that accompanied or supported the groups, represent a significant enterprise of the churches. In the late nineteenth century the education of working men – and to a lesser extent women – was driven by university extension programmes, the trade unions and the cooperative movement; the intended outcome was what one might call politically and socially educated citizens, motivated to improve their lot and share more fully in society. Much adult education during this period was geared towards literacy, and beyond that, education initiatives for the masses were often via large lecture series, often for 150–500 people at a time. However, at the turn of century, after the establishment of universal elementary education, there was a widespread revived interest in adult education, and fresh thinking about education accompanied it.

Perhaps the Workers' Educational Association (WEA), inaugurated in 1905, epitomizes the model and mood here. Albert Mansbridge, its founder, established smaller units for education, usually called tutorial classes, 'consisting of a sufficiently small number of members to allow of close intercourse between teacher and student'. These were often 30–40 in number though in many areas they functioned with far fewer members. The small group developed as a forum for such education in part because of the small numbers involved in many places, and in part because the model allowed for participation. Thus people learned to form and express themselves in the interchange with teacher and peers.

The link of the WEA to the churches was strong. Albert Mansbridge was a lay preacher in the Church of England. William Temple, later Archbishop of Canterbury, was the WEA's first president and R. H. Tawney, a leading figure in the movement, described his tutorial classes as a form of 'fellowship' with his students. This thirst for education and the models that accompanied it influenced the churches. Clearly many of the small-group programmes set up by the churches were educational in intention and often focused on social issues such as poor law, housing, model factories and health. Books were produced, lectures given, and small groups worked through programmes with trained group leaders.[3] The style of other church programmes was similarly orientated towards learning. The Wesley Guild, for example, was set up as a young people's movement in 1896 by the Wesleyan Methodist Church, for a combination of devotional, literary and social purposes. The Guild became established in almost every circuit and local church. Its standard structure was a lecture followed by questions and discussion, with the aim of 'the diligent culture of the mind' in order to give 'God thoughtful and intelligent service'.[4] In the same way most Bible studies would have been led by the clergy or trained lay preachers, and the basic aim was the imparting of information so that members were better equipped in understanding and acting on their faith. While it will be true that devotional practices and attitudes would have been the main concern of many church groups, the influence of the study circle or adult learning class was a key influence on the form and feel of small groups in church during this time. This drive towards being better educated continued to influence small-group activity at least until the Second World War.

1940–70: house groups

In his 1969 book *House Groups* Michael Skinner states that he has been an unashamed fanatic for house groups for over 25 years.[5] This locates his first embrace of house groups around 1944. It is quite difficult to identify the exact start of the widespread use of the term 'house group' in the life of the churches in the UK; though since it is hard to find any reference in the literature much earlier than the Second World War, it can reasonably be assumed that the groups were a post-war development. This

---

3 For example, the Congregational Union ran a group-leaders programme for its study and service programmes – see *The 1919 Report*, p. 252.

4 John A. Vickers, *Dictionary of Methodism in Britain and Ireland*, Peterborough: Epworth Press, 2000, p. 383. This is paralleled in other churches by organizations such as Christian Endeavour and the Mothers' Union.

5 M. J. Skinner, *House Groups*, London: Epworth Press, 1969, Preface.

does not mean that the practice did not exist before 1940. Having a small Christian group in a home has been a recurring form of Christian gathering and has always been an option for dissidents, minorities and renewal movements[6] – but the use of the term itself as signifying an established pattern within regular church life does not seem to have entered the vocabulary until the middle of the twentieth century. Indeed when Michael Skinner was developing a house-group system at Elvet Methodist Church, Durham, in the 1960s, it was still seen as new and innovative. It may well be that the baby-boomer generation, those who came to adulthood in the 1960s, found house groups most attractive.

House groups can be characterized as more democratic, more participatory and more pastoral than study groups. While often developed from the older Bible-study groups, prayer groups and study circles, they drew on new forms and patterns that were emerging in the post-war culture and responded to the crises and needs of the same period.

There were probably a number of factors that influenced this development.

First, the modern ecumenical movement was a significant force in British churches after 1945 and promoted meetings for cooperation, mutual understanding and exchange. While the beginning of this movement is usually traced to the 1910 Edinburgh Missionary Conference, the impact of the movement at the level of local church life was not felt until after the Second World War.[7] The British Council of Churches sponsored small study-group initiatives to address particular issues in church life or society, such as the 1966 The People Next Door programme and, later, the hugely successful 1980s Lenten studies that attracted large numbers to small groups.[8]

---

6 For a number of examples through history, see chapter 3 in Robert and Julia Banks, *The Church Comes Home*, Peabody, MA: Hendrickson, 1998.

7 The British Council of Churches was inaugurated in 1942, the World Council of Churches in 1948 and the Church of South India in 1947.

8 In 1986, Inter-Church Process sponsored a Lent Course entitled 'What on Earth is the Church for?'. A million people and 57 radio stations took part and between 60,000 and 70,000 small groups met. A similar programme was mounted in 1988, entitled 'Who on Earth Are You?'.

The word 'study' here is, however, misleading: the central dynamic of many of these meetings was not the accumulation of knowledge in itself but the breaking down of prejudice, the mutual understanding of traditions and recognition of what Christians had in common. It depended on Christians meeting each other with a degree of openness and a desire for some reconciliation and building of relationships. The small-group format both expressed and extended these attitudes.

However, the ecumenical movement did not invent house groups; rather, they drew on patterns emerging from other sources. A second tributary to the house-group phenomenon was the wider societal interest in small groups. Research and study of small groups began early in the twentieth century, but again popular appropriation of the values and insights of small-group sociology only really began in the middle of the century. One of the most significant developments, as I mentioned in the previous chapter, was the formation of Alcoholics Anonymous (AA) in the early 1940s. This was in effect a small-group approach to the problem of alcoholism, built on the conviction that individuals could be cured with support and the accountability framework sustained by the group itself. In other words, AA was a success because it harnessed the therapeutic power of a small group. Interestingly, the founders drew much from an earlier Christian small-group movement in the 1920s and 1930s known as the Oxford Group. Its founder, Frank Buchman, a Lutheran Pastor, started the movement in 1921 with an organization called A First Century Christian Fellowship. The Oxford Group movement worked on the idea that change is achieved by inward transformation facilitated by confession, conversion, honesty and divine activity. It promoted practices – often called the four absolutes – of honesty, purity, unselfishness and love. Alcoholics Anonymous took the ideas of honest accountability, mutual guarding and positive regard from the Oxford Group movement and integrated them into an effective rehabilitation process.

T-groups also arose in the 1940s. These small groups, sometimes called Human Relations Training groups or Encounter groups, drew on group psychotherapy, so that participants learned about themselves and about small-group processes through their interactions with each other. With the aid of a facilitator, participants were encouraged to share emotional reactions that arose in response to their fellow participants' actions and statements and thus to grow in self-awareness of the impact of one's behaviour on others. Developed by Kurt Lewin and promoted by Carl Rogers, these groups were widely influential.[9]

The therapeutic uses of small groups affected the churches' training programmes and they were employed in some forms of ministry, especially chaplaincy and mental-health work, rather than directly feeding the pattern of house groups. Indeed for many the idea of personal exposure or accountability within a small group was not attractive. Nevertheless the general idea that small groups were somehow good for you; that people could help one another along; that small groups could facilitate healing and reconciliation, fed into house-group development and worked to complement the agenda of the ecumenical movement. Churches sometimes organized their church community into geographical areas, where one or more house groups met, and assumed that much of the pastoral work would be carried by the small group, at least in caring for members and sometimes in supporting those in need in their local area.

To recognize that the pastoral dimension, fed by the therapeutic interest in small groups, was stronger in the house groups than the earlier study circles is not to deny the continued value of learning through small groups. House groups were often set up to study but the pedagogical form and dynamic at work within them was changing during this middle period. In particular the idea that people are active in the construction of their own knowledge began to filter out from Jean Piaget's work on child development. What had been found to be broadly true of children's learning, namely that it proceeds through a process of assimilation (fitting new experiences into one's world view) and accommodation (altering your world view or frame for seeing reality), was gradually seen to apply to all human beings throughout life. Just as

---

9 Carl R. Rogers, *Encounter Groups*, Harmondsworth: Penguin, 1985 [1970].

some schools began to experiment with the Harkness method of tutorial discussion, in which the teacher plays a kind of facilitation role so that all members of the group can contribute to the discussion and develop their understanding, so house groups were shaped into meetings where all were encouraged to participate actively.

Thus house groups were being shaped by both therapeutic and educational developments in wider society. They existed in two main forms during this period. In many parishes, especially from the 1960s onwards, small house groups were used for the six weeks of Lent. This was a natural structure for ecumenical meetings of local church members, as noted above, for it involved a limited time commitment, and many Anglican and some Catholic parishes already had an established form others could use. The other type was a more or less permanent group attached to one church. These were mainly developed by the free churches and Evangelical Anglicans. In all types, the structure was to gather at the home of a member (possibly but not necessarily that of the leader), share some simple refreshment such as tea and biscuits, discuss issues arising out of a Bible passage, book or specially prepared material, with prayer at the opening and closing of the meeting. Sometimes this prayer was offered by the leader and sometimes shared by all members in the open extempore style of prayer meetings.

This pattern of small-group work was also used increasingly in membership or confirmation preparation, in youth groups and for occasional projects or programmes.

It would be unfair to imply that theological and ecclesial thinking was not a factor in the shaping of house groups. Hans-Ruedi Weber wrote an influential article in 1957 entitled 'The Church in the House' that described a thriving Protestant church in Italy meeting in a home prior to the completion of its church building. The picture painted of the integration of the sacred and secular, the deep sense of participation, including an interactive preaching dialogue, and the feeling of fellowship caused the author to suggest that much might be lost when the building was finished and to encourage people not to think of the house as a temporary expedient but a full expression of ecclesial life.[10] Likewise H. Kraemer's *Theology of the Laity*, published a year later, advocated the development of small Christian cells as a counter to lack of community,[11] and John A. T. Robinson described the development of the house church as the single most important new thing happening in the Church of England in 1960.[12] It may be fair to say, however, that this thinking had more impact in the next wave of ecclesial life as new forces contributed to the development of church-based small groups.

1960–2000: groups for mission and discipleship

In the 1960s two extraordinary small-group phenomena began that were to impact churches in the UK and across the world. One came from Latin America, the other from Korea. Although neither would be noticed widely for another decade, both carried worldwide influence and inspired new approaches to both mission and small groups. The first was called the 'base Christian communities', the second 'cell church'.

Base Christian communities

Base Christian communities (BCCs) were advocated at the Conference of Latin American Bishops in Medellín in Colombia in 1968. The intention that the final document makes clear was to develop small communities that would be in solidarity with the poor of Latin and South America against the oppressive structures and practices of the elite of the region.

---

10 Hans-Ruedi Weber, 'The Church in the House', originally printed in *Laity* in 1957 and reprinted in the Anabaptist series of *Concern Pamphlets*, no. 5 (June 1958), pp. 7–28.

11 H. Kraemer, *The Theology of the Laity*, London: Lutterworth Press, 1958.

12 John A. T. Robinson, *Essays on Being the Church in the World*, London: SCM Press, 1960.

It is necessary that small basic communities be developed in order to establish a balance with minority groups, which are the groups in power ... The Church – the People of God – will lend its support to the downtrodden of every social class so that they might come to know their rights and how to make use of them.

In reality some of these communities were already in existence in 1968, but the Bishops' Conference promoted and strengthened them. By 1982 it was reported that there were over 150,000 such groups established in Latin America.[13] Their structure and practice is reflected in the series of recorded conversations by Ernesto Cardenal in Nicaragua. As the small group in Solentiname gathered for Mass, often in someone's hut, they had a dialogue on the Gospel for the day with the priest rather than a homily. Here is an extract on the Parable of the Mustard Seed (Matthew 13.31–45):

WILLIAM said: 'That's why he compares it with a mustard seed. Because instead of the kingdom of worldwide power, which the Jews were waiting for (which was a reactionary idea), the kingdom of Jesus is shown as a very humble little group, which goes unnoticed at the beginning: a carpenter with a few poor people. Among his disciples he didn't have one important person. Later it will also be a political kingdom that will control the earth, and that's why he says it will be greater than all the trees. But at the beginning it was an invisible kingdom.'

And TERRESITA, William's wife, with her son Juan in her arms, said: 'The truth is that the kingdom belongs to the poor, and that's why it's unnoticed at first. But the poor will control the world and will possess the earth.'

LAUREANO: 'And you can say the same about the revolution: at the beginning nobody notices it. It's little groups, cells.'

CORONEL URTECHO: 'Like this little group now that's telling us things in Solentiname.' And he added after a pause: 'On the other hand, there are ostentatious works of the church, created

13 David Prior, *The Church in the Home*, Basingstoke: Marshall Pickering, 1983, p. 15.

with great pride, that give promise of being great things, and end up in nothing. They are the opposite of the kingdom of God, like the Jesuit Central-American University.'

LAUREANO: 'And the guerrilla groups are small, insignificant, poor. And they're often wiped out. But they're going to change society. Can't we apply also to them the parable of the mustard seed?'

MARCELINO, with his calm voice said: 'I don't know about the mustard seed, but I do know about the *guasima* seed, which is tiny. I'm looking at that *guasima* tree over there. It's very large, and the birds come to it too. I say to myself: that's what we are, this little community a *guasima* seed. It doesn't seem there's any connection between the thing that's round and tiny, like a pebble, and that great big tree. It doesn't seem either that there's any connection between some poor *campesinos* and a just and well-developed society, where there is an abundance and everything is shared. And we are the seed of that society. But I know we are a seed and not a pebble.'[14]

This potent mixture of piety, poverty and political conscious-ness marks many of these conversations and illustrates well the orientation of the groups. Often established among the poor, they carried a wave of social and political empowerment. They were closely allied with liberation theology and the educational work of Paolo Freire. As their stories became known, many Christians in the USA and Europe were inspired to similar kinds of enter-prise: small groups for the transformation of unjust systems and resistance to the destructive effects of the capitalist agenda.

In the main, however, BCCs have not been 'successful' on a large scale in the UK or other parts of the western world in terms of replicating the structure and patterns witnessed in Latin America. They continue to exert some influence on the Roman Catholic Church and there are interesting examples of what are now often called 'small Christian communities' (SCCs) reported

14 Ernesto Cardenal, *The Gospel in Solentiname, Vol. 2*, New York: Orbis Books, 1985, pp. 53–4.

from the UK.[15] The solidarity with the poor has not been a widespread motivation for small Christian groups or communities as it was in the originating impulse for BCCs, though it may have reminded Christians in the West of the centrality of this theme in the Scriptures.[16] Its main influence may have been in stimulating a mission-orientated way of thinking about small Christian gatherings. It is interesting that David Prior's influential book *The Church in the Home*, published in 1983, draws inspiration from the BCCs and other small groups in the developing world.[17] Indeed his book is structured around a statement made in the Archdiocese of Vitória, Brazil and drawn up by these grassroots communities for the guidance of other BCCs. He sees in these communities, often meeting in small groups, a recovery of gospel truths for the Church in the UK.[18] There is a combination of evangelical zeal and passion for justice at the heart of the Vitória statement.

The Church is like a bus. No one gets on a bus to walk up and down it but to be carried from one place to another. A church is a vehicle as well, one that carries us towards the Kingdom of God. The mission of the church doesn't lie within itself, but outside it. It is to proclaim the presence of the Kingdom of God within the world of men. No one talks for his own benefit but to be heard by others. So the Church lives and preaches the gospel to transform the world, and to transform men ...

In the Bible a prophet isn't somebody who foretells the future. He is someone who points out to others what the will of God really is. That is the vocation of the Church in each ecclesial community: to show people what really is God's will. It is

---

15 Joseph G. Healey and Jeanne Hinton, *Small Christian Communities Today: Capturing the New Moment*, Maryknoll, NY: Orbis, 2005; see esp. chapters 12 and 13. There are also BCCs in various parts of Europe, described in chapter 11.

16 David Sheppard, *Bias to the Poor*, London: Hodder & Stoughton, 1983.

17 Prior, *Church in the Home*.

18 Prior, *Church in the Home*; See appendix A 'The Church the People Want', p. 162. The document is not dated but is clearly before 1983, when Prior's book was published.

not the will of the powerful, who only want to give orders and increase their wealth. It is the will of Jesus Christ, who made himself poor among the poor. Just like Jesus, the community ought to denounce the mistakes and injustices committed by society. When a Christian is silent, then God is silent because he wants to speak through our mouths.

Justice and Peace groups in the UK often cite BCCs as their inspiration but it is difficult for many of them to be outside their middle-class starting point and identify fully with the context of poverty in which these small groups arose. The form of working for justice demonstrated by Christians in the West has been very different. Campaigns such as Jubilee 2000, Drop the Debt, Action on Climate Change and Tax Justice are conducted through networks and partnerships within and beyond churches and are not dependent on the kind of small-group Bible study and empowerment at the heart of their Latin American counterparts. However, BCCs did stimulate an active missional agenda that focused on social justice and the transformation of society.

Cell church

The other major movement, cell church, began in Korea in the mid-1960s at the Yoido Full Gospel Church. This Assemblies of God church is now reckoned to be the largest church in the world with over 800,000 members, and it attributes its success to the development of a small-group system.[19] After working to the point of exhaustion in 1964, Paul – now David – Yonggi Cho, the pastor, began a system of home-based cell groups covering Metropolitan Seoul. This restructuring was primarily for small-group Bible study but developed into a means of evangelism and the nurture of new Christians. It rapidly expanded. By 1980 the church congregation was 141,000 strong and has continued to grow to its present size with a cell-group system that now numbers tens of thousands of groups. The book published by Paul Cho

---

19 'O come all ye faithful', *The Economist*, 1 November 2007.

on cell multiplication has been influential in promoting this vision and similar stories of phenomenal growth have been recounted in Singapore, South America and North America.[20]

The central emphasis in this approach is the notion of a cell group as being like the biological cell of, say, the human body. There are two aspects of biological cells that are particularly high-lighted. First, a cell contains the DNA that defines the species and, second, cells will naturally multiply. Some advocates extend this metaphor to include other cell functions such as community (the importance of interaction with other cells), outreach (preparation of nutrients for other parts of the body via the Golgi apparatus) and protection (the lysosomes that deal with waste and repair).[21] The crucial analogy is, however, the essential nature of the cell and its ability to replicate and grow other cells. The kind of small group envisaged is, and needs to see itself as, church, not a feature or element of church. John Banks calls this 'embodying rather than extending' the Church.[22] That is, a cell will be the primary location of church for its members and will contain within itself all that it means to be church. Coming together with others in celebration is desirable, but church exists already in the small group, and as such it should do the work of the Church, par-ticularly in evangelism and outreach. The cell will be the place to invite non-Christians, disciple people in the way of Jesus, wor-ship, learn and serve and thus grow the Church.

While there are several versions of cell church, and some are more rigidly structured and demanding than others, the form of cell that has been most influential in the UK has largely come

20 Paul Yonggi Cho, *Successful Home Cell Groups*, Plainfield, NJ: Logos International, 1981. For the stories of cell success from various parts of the world, see Ralph W. Neighbour, *Where Do We Go from Here? A Guidebook for the Cell Group Church*, Houston, TX: Touch Publications, 1990, pp. 23–36 and B. Donahue and R. Robinson, *Building a Church of Small Groups*, Grand Rapids, MI: Zondervan, 2001. On the development of cell church in Argentina, see also Juan Carlos Ortiz and Jamie Buckingham, *Call to Discipleship*, Plain-field, NJ: Logos International, 1975.

21 Ron Trudinger, *Cells for Life*, Eastbourne: Kingsway, 1983, pp. 29–33.

22 John Banks, *Group: See How They Run: House Fellowship, the House Church, Class Meetings, the Cell*, London: Epworth Press, 1967.

through Cell UK, set up in 1995 by Laurence Singlehurst.[23] Through its five core values, Cell UK was able to articulate a vision of all Christians engaged in mission, and as with BCCs, one of the key attractions of cell to many church leaders was the missionary orientation of the group. However, where people had not been able to imagine how BCCs could operate in the mainstream of western Christianity, many people saw how cells could be transplanted into British soil and related to existing churches.

Cell UK has worked by providing two key resources for churches to develop cell groups. First, it delivered a core set of five key values for groups to adopt and, second, it offered a simple structure to express these values in a working pattern for every group meeting.

The core values are as follows:

Each cell/small group is based around the following beliefs/ values:

- Jesus is at the centre of the gathered believers and the individual Christian's life.
- Christian community is fostered through relationship.
- Each member can grow in their Christian walk and knowledge of God.
- Every member can be released to minister to others in the Body of Christ.
- Every member can seek to bring others to Christ.[24]

The structure for cell meetings is known as 'the 4Ws'. This is summarized as follows by Cell UK:

- **Welcome** – involving some sort of 'icebreaker' question for members, who in turn all give their response. 'Each member

---

23 See William K. Kay, *Apostolic Networks in Britain: New Ways of Being Church*, Milton Keynes: Paternoster, 2007, pp. 191–202 for a discussion of the influence of shepherding and the G12 approaches in cells in the new churches.

24 www.celluk.org.uk/about/whatiscell.php. For a slightly different articulation of the values using an 'ABCDE' mnemonic, see Phil Potter, *The Challenge of Cell Church: Getting to Grips with Cell Church Values*, Oxford: Bible Reading Fellowship, 2001.

participates from the outset, hears their own voice in the meeting and feels included from the start rather than spectating.'

- **Worship** – in some form with or without music.
- **Word** – that is a study and application of a teaching, perhaps from the Sunday service, Bible passage or other source. Often at this point there will be opportunity for corporate prayer for those who request it and an opportunity for the cell members to minister one to another.
- **Witness** – focused on mission and in particular how to serve and share the good news with non-Christian friends, work colleagues and neighbours often leading into planning strategy and prayer.

The value of this structure has been twofold. First, it has enabled leaders to involve many members in leading some part of the meeting. Thus the leader becomes more of a facilitator, drawing others into leadership on a weekly basis. Second, it has kept people thinking about how to live Christian-ly and how to communicate faith to others. Rather than a Bible study or discussion that could easily end with no immediate practical outcome, cells are structurally orientated towards application, witness and outreach.

Accurate figures on cells and cell churches in the UK are difficult to come by, but the vocabulary is widely recognized and used in churches across most denominations, with the possible exception of Roman Catholic and Orthodox churches. In my study of churches in the north-east of England over a third identified themselves as having cells or seeking to be cell churches.

The impact of cell churches on small groups in the UK is significant, both directly and indirectly, but its story has been interwoven with two other movements in church life, namely the charismatic movement and the rise of the new churches.

The charismatic movement

The charismatic movement also began in the 1960s. Usually traced to Dennis Bennett in Van Nuys, California, the movement is broadly the incorporation of phenomena associated with Pentecostal churches, such as being filled with the Spirit and spiritual gifts, into the main stream denominations of the Protestant – and later Catholic – churches, creating another stream of spirituality alongside evangelical, liberal, high church and radical. In the UK this was associated with the ministries of Anglicans such as David Watson and Michael Harper and promoted by the Fountain Trust.

One of the outcomes of the movement has been both to increase the number and develop the role of small groups. Initially this was much to do with the nurture of a new kind of spirituality both unfamiliar and threatening to traditional worship services. If the inclusion of the use of charismatic gifts in worship was too divisive – and it often was – then a small group of more sympathetic members was a good place to start. The small group provided a safer place to explore the experience and, for some, a way of surviving the hostility with which others in the church greeted this new brand of Christian faith. In my own research, a new-church leader related his story of being in a Methodist church, when the local minister was touched by charismatic renewal. While this did not receive a warm welcome in most of the churches of the circuit, the minister gathered a small group, before he left for another appointment, to lay hands on them and prophesy that this group would be the source of renewal for the church. The group continued to meet regularly to use charismatic gifts, to seek visions and prophesies and to support each other, but the local churches in the area by and large remained untouched. He described the small group as his means of survival for several years until the new churches began to emerge, and he could make the transfer to a Christian community that valued and used his new-found spirituality.

Small groups also work with the grain and intention of charismatic spirituality, for even where a large church gathering encourages the use of spiritual gifts in worship, the number able to participate is limited by time and structure, and contribution is often restricted to leading figures or a few more extrovert types. The high degree of participation by all requires a small number, and meetings of 8 to 15 people mean that most, if not all, can contribute. Another person I interviewed described small groups as enabling the 'charismatication' of the church, by which he meant that small groups' numbers and interaction provided a way of ensuring all could experience and use gifts in worship and ministry to others.

Stephen Hunt sees the use of Alpha and the small groups that result from it as a measurement of the impact and spread of charismatic Christianity.[25] This connection between the charismatic movement and Alpha is taken much further by Tony Watling.[26] He underlines, extends and reinforces the view of Hunt that Alpha has roots in and is part of the movement for charismatic renewal. Much of his evidence is drawn from his empirical research on Alpha courses in Scotland. He argues that Alpha is an initiation into a charismatic world view that, once adopted, is embodied and performed within charismatic church meetings and services. His main argument for this conclusion is the centrality of the Holy Spirit weekend in the Alpha structure and the way it is experienced in practice. He likens the focus on the Spirit (Session 10), and especially the weekend, to the 'ministry times' of John Wimber. His records of the Holy Spirit weekends demonstrate the charismatic nature of the key events, including speaking in tongues and other gifts of the Spirit. He also uses McGuire's characteristics of the charismatic world view to show how it is prefigured in Alpha and how Alpha acts as a portal or ritual entry point into it.[27] He concludes that small groups may be a key ingredient to continue to maintain the world view.[28]

For these reasons the charismatic movement has tended to extend the use of small groups in church communities. The evidence is that charismatic influence on the longer established

---

25 Stephen Hunt, 'The Alpha Programme: Some Tentative Observations of the State of the Art: Evangelism in the UK', *Journal of Contemporary Religion* 18:1 (2003), p. 81.

26 Tony Watling, 'Experiencing Alpha: Finding and Embodying the Spirit and Being Transformed – Empowerment and Control in a (Charismatic) Worldview', *Journal of Contemporary Religion* 20:1 (2005).

27 Meredith B. McGuire, *Pentecostal Catholics: Power, Charisma, and Order in a Religious Movement*, Philadelphia, PA: Temple University Press, 1982.

28 Watling, 'Experiencing Alpha', p. 96.

denominations has been to enlarge the role of and give a new dynamic to small groups. In a study examining the influence of the movement on 3,120 Anglican churches, Leslie Francis et al. concluded that 'The major structural change in local church life brought about by the charismatic movement, according to the present data, concerns growth in the number of adults supporting house groups.'[29]

The new churches

The new churches in the UK are sometimes included in what is known as 'third-wave Pentecostalism',[30] but as Andrew Walker has pointed out, the early development of the new churches predates the charismatic movement in that the notion of a 'Restorationist Church' was being articulated by Arthur Wallis and Campbell McAlpine before 1960, whereas the UK charismatic movement is usually dated from about 1964 with the setting up of the Fountain Trust and had its heyday in the 1970s.[31] In reality these were caught up together and both were influenced by cell-church advocates in the 1970s.

The new churches have been given at least three designations. Originally called House Churches because their early meetings were often in homes, they have also been described as Restorationist Churches and Network Churches, though the term new churches is widely used both by the churches themselves and by their older denominational contemporaries. The names are important for understanding these rapidly growing churches. 'Restorationism' points to the vision that has united many of these churches – a vision of a restored (non-denominational)

29 Leslie J. Francis, David W. Lankshear and Susan H. Jones, 'The Influence of the Charismatic Movement on Local Church Life: A Comparative Study among Anglican Rural, Urban and Suburban Churches', *Journal of Contemporary Religion* 15:1 (2000), p. 129.

30 C. Peter Wagner, 'Third Wave', in S. M. Burgess and E. M. van der Maas (eds), *The New International Dictionary of Pentecostal and Charismatic Movements*, Grand Rapids, MI: Zondervan, 2002.

31 Andrew Walker, *Restoring the Kingdom: The Radical Christianity of the House Church Movement*, London: Hodder & Stoughton, 1985, pp. 35–47.

New Testament Church. There is among the leaders of the new churches a conviction that God was speaking afresh to people in the late twentieth century, recalling them to reclaim key New Testament truths. Central to these restored truths was the idea of the fivefold ministry of Ephesians 4: apostles, prophets, evangelists, pastors and teachers. In particular the role of apostle as divinely appointed for founding and overseeing churches – what Walker calls charismatic episcope – marks a distinctive ecclesiology and has led to a network association of churches under the oversight of one of the leading figures.

The growth and development of new churches has been considerable over the past 40 years, and they too have contributed to the growth in small-group activity in churches. William Kay[32] reported that the majority of new churches have either house groups or cell groups, and belonging to a small group is an essential, expected part of belonging to the Church.

New-church websites tend to emphasize the centrality of the small groups, albeit in very user-friendly language.

> Small Groups are at the heart of [name] Vineyard and are a fun and relaxed way to become part of our family. They meet during the week in people's homes and involve meeting with God and just being together as friends. They are a place where we can build relationships, help and encourage one another, and learn what it means to have a loving God and be a loving people.

Being part of a small group has become for many new churches an essential aspect of ecclesiology, so much so that Helen Cameron identifies the 'small-group church' as one of the new cultural forms of church apparent in contemporary society.[33]

In my research I interviewed the senior pastor of one of the large and growing Network Churches in the north of England, where over 90 per cent of the 300-strong worshipping community

---

32 Kay, *Apostolic Networks in Britain*.

33 Helen Cameron, *Resourcing Mission: Practical Theology for Changing Churches*, London: SCM Press, 2010, pp. 24–37.

belonged to small groups. He described the purpose of these cells as:

> to provide a complementary experience of church, and ... the basic vision for church is fellowship, discipleship, and mission: Fellowship meaning fellowship first of all with God, and that involves worship and praise and so on; discipleship means growing people in the faith; and mission means reaching out to others ... I think we would probably say that the focus of cell groups is more on discipleship; to some extent on fellowship, which is both worship and just being in supportive relationship with each other; probably less so on mission – as I said, a 'keep-net' as opposed to a fishing-rod.

If discipleship language is the key to the work of the cells, it is clear in what follows that discipleship is to be understood in a missional not a pastoral framework.

> We use the word discipleship in contrast to being pastoral, I think, quite deliberately. Most people in church, I think, have a tendency towards the mentality that 'God is there to solve my problems', and so small groups become a place where my problems are shared and halved and therefore dealt with, and there's a big place for that and an important place for that kind of pastoral care. But discipleship language maintains the edge that the Christian life is a journey, that God has an agenda and a purpose which is not solving my problems, but engaging me and us in his purpose and his mission.[34]

Walker suggests that this emphasis on discipleship or 'discipling' indicates that the demands and expectations on believers are higher than most other churches, including the Pentecostals.

> The aim of discipleship is not to bring everyone into line but to ensure that all (including apostles) are open to correction and admonition within loving relationships.[35]

---

34 Interview, December 2010.
35 Walker, *Restoring the Kingdom*, pp. 145ff.

This expectation of high personal lifestyle standards and the accompanying accountability is achieved in small groups and gives small groups in new churches a particular flavour and orientation. This emphasis in turn has influenced how others see and speak of discipleship and small groups.

The new landscape and language of small groups

Some things should be clear from this overview of church small groups in the twentieth century. First, the form and structure of small groups has changed over the last 100 years. Although small groups have taken a wide variety of forms, one can detect significant shifts in the underlying orientation from the early to the middle and from the middle to the late part of the century.

Second, small groups have changed as wider society has changed. The interest in education as increasing personal knowledge, improving oneself and for the transformation of society that characterized the WEA (see p. 87), was mirrored in small church groups in the first decades after 1900. Learning as participation in knowledge creation and therapeutic encounter was a feature of the middle period, as it was in educational and medical settings. In the last part of our era the emphasis has shifted to learning for the outcomes of discipleship and mission. This is not surprising in an era that stresses educational and business outcomes as the basis for planning and resource allocation, and several researchers have attempted to understand the small-group phenomenon at the beginning of the twenty-first century through the business lens of George Ritzer's McDonaldization theory, which I discuss further in the next chapter.[36]

---

36 Hunt, 'The Alpha Programme'. David Harvey, 'Cell Church: Its Situation in British Evangelical Culture', in David A. Harvey (ed.), *A Contextual and Theological Examination of the British Cell Church Movement* [Electronic Resource], Sheffield: University of Sheffield, 2004; George Ritzer, *The McDonaldization of Society: An Investigation into the Changing Character of Contemporary Social Life*, Thousand Oaks, CA, London and New Delhi: Pine Forge Press, 1996.

Third, the general trend over the century has been to increase the use of small groups in churches. While new forms of small groups have been born, other forms have continued, perhaps to meet an ever widening range of spiritual needs. According to a 2001 churches survey, 37 per cent of English churchgoers questioned said they belonged to a small group for prayer or Bible study, and only one per cent said that in their church there was no opportunity to join a small group.[37] In addition to the expanding number and types of small group, the range of material online and in print continues to spiral. Explosion is not an inappropriate word to use to highlight the growing significance of small groups at the beginning of the twenty-first century. While church attendance continues to fall, the numbers involved in small groups as a proportion of those attending church is higher than ten years ago and looks set to increase further.

Finally, the Church's rationale for small groups has also changed over the period. The books, papers and leaflets accompanying the various phases have offered their reasons for small groups on different theological, pastoral or missiological grounds. This surely reflects both the situation in which the Church finds itself in each period and changing concepts of what it means to be a follower of Jesus. Currently we are in the climate of the Church's recovery of mission, and increasingly that is manifest in discipleship formation, seen as missional spirituality and bringing others to faith.

We will discuss in later chapters whether this concept of mission is sufficient and whether the new forms of small group realize or only aspire to these notions.

---

37 *Faith in Life*, London: Churches' Information for Mission, 2001.

7

Research on Church-related Small Groups

What I described as a small-group explosion in the last chapter has, not surprisingly, attracted the attention of researchers. Particularly in the last 20 years the phenomenon of church-related small groups has been of interest to sociologists of religion, who have asked questions such as: Why do people join these small groups? What do they get out of them? What are the effects on members who participate in small groups? What are the effects on the church communities of people participating in small groups? What are the intentions and goals of churches in pursuing a small groups' programme and have these been realized? Why has the increased interest in small groups arisen at this time?

In this chapter we will review some of the research findings and the reflections on these findings. It is not a technical review, thus I will not discuss in any detail the methodology or scrutinize the robustness of the research. You will find references to the academic papers and books in the footnotes in case you want to read and explore the research in more depth. I will gather the findings under three areas:

- micro level – research about particular small groups;
- middle level – research about churches with small groups;
- macro level – research about church small groups in the wider culture.

First, a health warning about research and its methods!

Research on small groups can be carried out in 'laboratory

conditions'. That is, an artificial simulation is set up to see what happens when certain conditions or factors are altered. Some research on small groups has been done in this form in the past, particularly over questions around leadership, but in the main this approach has not been used to study church-related small groups. These are studied 'in the field' through observation or by asking questions of those who belong to a small group, the group leaders and/or their church leaders. The main tools have been question-naires, interviews and case studies. There are very good reasons for these approaches in that they better reflect real-world experi-ence and the ordinary functioning of these small groups, but like all research tools they are not perfect and present some difficulty for the researcher in: getting to the data; deciding whether the data truly reflects the reality it seeks to understand; interpreting the data for others. For example, if you want to observe what happens at a small group, you need to be present at its meet-ings or record them in some way. In both cases you introduce another element into the group, either a person or a recording device such as a video or audio recorder that may make people more self-conscious and thus change their behaviour. Likewise, if a researcher interviews someone their subliminal body language may affect the kinds of answers the interviewee gives. And we all know about questionnaires that our answers can depend on the mood we are in at that moment and how we read or hear the questions. After helping devise and design questionnaires for 15 years, it never ceases to amaze me that when a questionnaire is put to people (in a pilot test if you are fortunate), a question that was perfectly clear and unambiguous in the researcher's mind is understood quite differently by the person filling it in. There are many other difficulties to tackle, but suffice it for us to recognize that researching human behaviour is a tricky business and find-ings are indicative rather than an exact science.

Most research faces squarely the problems and uses approaches and methods that minimize the skewing of the data to give a reasonable picture of what is studied. The information is often made stronger and more accurate when different pieces of research are combined, when the study covers a large number of cases or is continued for a long time, and when the work is replicated in different contexts and settings.

Research and findings

Micro level: the small group

Some research has concentrated on understanding single instances of church-related small groups through individual case studies. Abby Day, for example, studied a baptist women's prayer group for several months. The pattern of the group meetings was a simple one of gathering on a Wednesday morning for coffee that flowed into 'chatting' and then focused in an organized and corporate prayer time, where people prayed for issues identified by the members. The 'chatting' was related to prayers said on previous occasions. They discussed whether the prayers were answered and if not, why not, and what they should pray for now. Day's conclusion was that these conversations, far from being incidental, were a vital form of the group process.

> If their previous prayers had not been answered in the way they had originally asked, they would pray for the same person or situation differently after discussion, adding a new dimension in the light of their newly acquired understanding.[1]

Although the women dismissed the chatting as preliminary to the 'real business' of prayer, Day saw this as 'the mechanism by which the group members resolved for themselves the apparent dissonance between what they had wanted and what has actually happened'. She interpreted the group as a mediating structure for faith and belief that enabled the women to engage in theology. It gave them a form of faith engagement not available in the gathered Sunday church context: 'during a service, they are in a position to accept or reject privately the theological insights or arguments

---

1 Abby Day, 'Doing Theodicy: An Empirical Study of a Women's Prayer Group', *Journal of Contemporary Religion* 20:3 (2005), p. 344.

being presented by their church leaders. But here, in their friend's home, they are "doing theology".'[2] She does not understand this group process negatively but rather positively, where the women are agents and active in their own faith development: 'the women were not resigning themselves passively to God's will, but expanding their view of God by constructing a theological response'.[3]

This small piece of research demonstrates the power of this particular group and, by implication, other groups to help people own and develop their own theology. Similar findings have emerged from other studies. For example, Peter Cahn studied Catholic members of a men's Alcoholics Anonymous (AA) group in Mexico[4] and discovered that over a period of time the men did not abandon or substitute AA for their received faith but that their AA group helped them revise and renew their conception of God and develop new – alcohol free – ways of participating in community-related events. Both these examples of small groups empowering personal faith stress the distance the group has from the official doctrine or practice of the Church. Indeed it is precisely this looser relationship to the institution that creates a safe space for individual honesty, experimentation and personal expressions of faith. In the growing research associated with Ordinary Theology[5] there are several examples of small groups allowing a similar degree of freedom and enabling confidence to express faith even where it appears 'unorthodox'.[6] In some situations the distance of the small group from a parent body enables not only ownership and freedom of creative theological thinking but the

---

2 Day, 'Doing Theodicy', p. 350.

3 Day, 'Doing Theodicy', p. 352.

4 Peter S. Cahn, 'Saints with Glasses: Mexican Catholics in Alcoholics Anonymous', *Journal of Contemporary Religion* 20:2 (2005), pp. 217–29.

5 Ordinary Theology is usually understood as 'the theology and theologizing of Christians who have received little or no theological education of a scholarly, academic or systematic kind'. Research then is exploring the way such adults 'articulate their religious understanding'. See Jeff Astley, *Ordinary Theology: Looking, Listening and Learning in Theology*, Explorations in Pastoral, Practical and Empirical Theology, Aldershot: Ashgate, 2002.

6 See, for example, Helen Savage, 'Ordinary Learning', in Jeff Astley and Leslie J. Francis (eds), *Exploring Ordinary Theology*, Farnham: Ashgate, 2013.

survival of minority views within a continued commitment to the larger body with different convictions.[7]

The other way of accessing the effects of small groups on their members is through surveys that seek group participants' responses to questions. These surveys tend not to attend to the detailed working or context of individual small groups but concentrate on the perceived impact on members' lives over a larger number of broadly similar types of group. So Robert Wuthnow's research project in the mid-1990s in the USA used a questionnaire with 1,000 small-group members. He discovered that 66 per cent felt closer to God as a result of their involvement in groups; 71 per cent said they were more able to forgive others; 55 per cent said it helped them share their faith with others outside the group; 69 per cent said it helped them serve others better. Some 84 per cent felt better about themselves because of being a member.

My own research in the north-east of England in 2010 found even higher levels of satisfaction by small-group members.[8] When asked to identify in what ways the group had helped them, 77 per cent thought it had made them more confident in their faith; 76 per cent said belonging to a group had made them more able to connect their faith and everyday life; 72 per cent said it had made them more accepting and forgiving of others; 79 per cent said it had strengthened their prayer life; 68 per cent said it had given them more confidence in speaking about their faith to others. The strongest response was that the group had brought them closer to God. A staggering 87 per cent of participants believed this, suggesting that the small group animates and empowers various aspects of what it means to be a Christian and to be in touch with God. These responses imply that members believe the small group is having a profound effect on their spirituality.

---

7 See Kathleen M. Joyce, 'The Long Loneliness: Liberal Catholics and the Conservative Church', in Robert Wuthnow (ed.), *I Come Away Stronger: How Small Groups are Shaping American Religion*, Grand Rapids, MI: Eerdmans, 1994.

8 A full report of the Leech research on church-related small groups in the North-East is to be added to the William Leech Fellowship website; see www. dur.ac.uk/m.j.masson/.

On the other hand, only about half thought that belonging to the group had made them more likely to help their neighbours (51 per cent). Even fewer thought that participation had got them more involved in justice issues on an international level (23 per cent); and only a few thought it had got them more involved in local issues such as loneliness and poverty (18 per cent). In this survey, small groups do not, necessarily, connect people more strongly to their neighbours or neighbourhoods, and issues of justice or local need are, at best, not more noticed or engaged with for most who attend the group – at worst they are seen as irrelevant or marginal to Christian discipleship.

Looking below the surface of these statistics is also revealing. For in my research, in a series of open questions where respondents were asked to describe how the group had affected them, a slightly different picture emerged. An analysis of the responses suggested that what people value most are the relational dynamics of the small group and the sense of pastoral support they receive. Some spoke of the group members as their 'true friends', others as their 'family'. Others expressed debt to their group for the way they had been helped through illness, challenging experience or personal tragedy, while many spoke of the sense of being supported and prayed for. A number said that the safe, secure and supporting atmosphere had enabled them to discover a new confidence, personal gifts and growth in leadership.

Similarly, when asked to identify the best part of belonging to a small group more than one in five used the word 'fellowship'. The next most popular word was 'friend' or 'friendship', 104 of 645 responses highlighting this notion. When one adds in those who said that being supported, getting to know or sharing with other people was the best part, then the majority of respondents are accounted for. By contrast, fewer than 40 mentioned the Bible, learning or study in their answer and the words 'mission', 'outreach', 'evangelism', 'serving' and 'neighbours' were not mentioned by anyone. When the words 'know' and 'knowing' were used they referred to the Bible or God 5 times and 54 times to knowing people. Clearly, the core of what was most beneficial to people was the relational experience at the heart of the meetings.

Taken together with the modest effects on individuals to get more involved with the neighbourhoods or issues of justice, it seems that people find an experience of community in small groups, within which they are able to search for God in deep and fulfilling ways. There is little evidence that the group experience pushes them to engage in or seek God in the more complex and contested areas of human society.

Middle level: the church with small groups

The research here is two-way. What effects do small groups have on a church community and how do church communities shape and influence their small groups?

The effect of small groups on religious communities

One line of research on small groups has been to explore what effect having small groups has on the faith communities in which they are situated. The questions are often to do with whether involvement in small groups increases or decreases the numbers attending places of worship and how small groups affect the corporate life of the religious community, its patterns of worship and learning.

Methods and approaches have tended to be quantitative, using surveys, national statistics and closed-interview questions so as to be able to make some form of measurable comparison. As measuring faith is notoriously difficult, other measures are used as indicative: how individuals feel about their church; how much money they give; what time they commit to their faith communities. So we know from surveys conducted among mega-churches – usually defined as churches with over 3,000 members – that a significant number of members have a sense of intimacy in their church, despite their congregation's size. Almost 50 per cent of those surveyed in 2001 thought the statement that 'church feels like a close-knit family' described their church very or quite well. This is usually explained by other statistical data – that 94 per cent of mega-churches have a small-group programme, and 50 per cent indicated that small groups are central to their strategy for Christian nurture and spiritual formation.[9] In short, small groups make large churches more intimate, personal and accessible.[10]

Research on church-connected small groups also suggests that those who join a group attend worship more often, feel a stronger connection to the church and give more time and money to the enterprise than those who do not belong to a small group.[11] Moreover small-group involvement is positively associated with individuals' commitment and participation in religious congregations, regardless of congregation size. Other researchers found that small groups in churches enhance racial-ethnic diversity,[12] promote congregational growth and have positive effects on members' beliefs and practices.[13] Of course, as Kevin Dougherty and Andrew Whitehead admit, these data indicate correlation not causation. It is not possible to argue from the data that attending a group increases the commitment to the church, giving of money and attendance at worship. It is quite possible that other factors such as personality type or already-held strong faith commitment will cause people to belong to a group and attend worship frequently. Dougherty and Whitehead tentatively venture that there may be a reinforcing cycle at work with small groups; that is, committed people will seek to belong to small groups, and

9 Source: Hartford Institute for Religious Research, Hartford Seminary, Hartford, CT.

10 Some research in 2011 suggests, however, that because mega-churches attract younger members in part for the anonymity they offer, it may over time be harder for them to get people into small groups. See Kevin D. Dougherty and Andrew L. Whitehead, 'A Place to Belong: Small Group Involvement in Religious Congregations', *Sociology of Religion* 72:1 (2011), pp. 91–111.

11 Dougherty and Whitehead, 'A Place to Belong'.

12 Kevin D. Dougherty, 'How Monochrome Is Church Membership? Racial-Ethnic Diversity in Religious Community', *Sociology of Religion* 64:1 (2003), pp. 65–85. Michael O. Emerson with Rodney M. Woo, *People of the Dream: Multiracial Congregations in the United States*, Princeton, NJ: Princeton University Press, 2006. Kevin D. Dougherty and R. Huyser, 'Racially Diverse Congregations: Organizational Identity and the Accommodation of Differences', *Journal for the Scientific Study of Religion* 47:1 (2008), pp. 23–44.

13 Nancy J. Martin, 'Small Groups in Big Churches', PhD thesis, University of Arizona, 2007.

belonging to one will nurture a stronger sense of commitment to the church.

How churches use and influence small groups

As we saw, in the study of individual groups, research found that the loose relationship of the small group to the sponsoring institution is one of the reasons it can help people own and develop their own faith. Of course, the small group itself will exert some pressure, and over time members tend to conform to a group set of norms, as we suggested in Chapter 5. In the church context this has been intentionally used to socialize new members into the values and practices of the church. Mathew Guest's congregational study of St Michael le Belfrey in York outlined the role of the small groups there as geared towards helping those who had attended Alpha courses to become more fully integrated into the congregation.[14] Its leaders were chosen, trained and supported with this purpose in mind, and groups were characterized by a form of socialization into the ethos of the congregation, with gentle policing of the boundaries of orthodoxy and initiation into the practices of charismatic Christianity. As they paid attention to the individual needs of the participants and provided emotional support, they were forging a shared charismatic evangelical identity.

Some researchers have seen this intentional promotion of particular values and the inculturation of individuals into a certain theological and religious world view through small groups as slightly sinister. Stephen Hunt's and Tony Watling's research referred to in Chapter 6 implies that Alpha is a major means of advancing charismatic Christianity in the Church, and David Harvey views cell church in a similar light, as promoting a church-growth strategy based on the cell churches of Asia and South America. The power of small groups to achieve this is through the implicit group pressure on members to conform to a group

---

14 Mathew Guest, *Evangelical Identity and Contemporary Culture: A Congregational Study in Innovation*, Studies in Evangelical History and Thought, Milton Keynes: Paternoster, 2007.

norm. My own case-study research suggests that overarching values of a sponsoring church are replicated in the church's small groups. In these cases only one of the three churches could be considered charismatic in orientation. An Anglican liberal catholic parish in the study held a central view of the Eucharist and desired to build up community in the parish. This was effectively achieved through a creative and energetic small-group programme. Its members owned and passed on core values in their meetings.[15] Daniel Olson obverses this same phenomenon in his study of the 'Disciple' programme at a United Methodist Church in a mid-western city of the USA.[16] The clearer these values are and the more visible they are in the church community, the more obvious they are in the small-group meetings.

Macro level: the church small-group phenomenon

Understanding how church small groups relate to the wider culture in which both the groups and the churches sit is difficult. As we noted earlier, some have seen the slightly macabre influence of modern business methods on the use of small groups in the church context. The so-called McDonaldization of the Church has been widely discussed.[17] This phrase, originally invented by George Ritzer, is a theory that some features of business practice have made for success in the global economy, in particular the fourfold principles of efficiency, calculability, predictability and control. Successful products are those that are optimized through these features and can be replicated elsewhere. Ritzer saw that these

---

15 See the chapter on Case Studies in the Leech research report at www.dur.ac.uk/m.j.masson/.

16 Daniel V. A. Olson, 'Making Disciples in a Liberal Protestant Church', in Wuthnow (ed.), *I Come Away Stronger*, pp. 125–47.

17 John William Drane, *The McDonaldization of the Church: Spirituality, Creativity, and the Future of the Church*, London: Darton, Longman & Todd, 2000; John Drane, *After McDonaldization*, London: Darton, Longman & Todd, 2008; Dennis Hayes and Robin Wynyard, *The McDonaldization of Higher Education*, Westport, CT and London: Bergin & Garvey, 2002; Barry Smart, *Resisting McDonaldization*, London: SAGE, 1999; Donna Dustin, *The McDonaldization of Social Work*, Aldershot: Ashgate, 2007.

principles were being applied to many other areas of society, and a number of writers believe they have been, consciously or unconsciously, transplanted into a church context. While it is likely that such a cross-fertilization takes place and that people in churches, as elsewhere, are often looking for the successful formula and proven strategy, it is only one aspect of the wider culture to affect small-groups practice in a Christian context. Also, this push factor from the churches is unlikely in itself to account for the growth in the popularity of small groups. There must be pull factors also.

The largest research project on small groups was that mentioned above headed by Robert Wuthnow in the mid-1990s in the USA.[18] This three-year project was under a team of 15 scholars. It surveyed more than 1,000 members of small groups and over 900 who did not belong to small groups. It also interviewed more than 100 members, leaders and clergy and did intensive case studies on 12 selected groups for between six months and three years.

Wuthnow's take on the cultural issues is different. Rather than discerning the hand of Christian entrepreneurs attempting to promote certain spiritualities or replicate growth patterns, he sees small groups as providing faith communities with a resource for responding to significant shifts in patterns of society and the understanding of faith.

The general findings of the survey were that the small-group movement was vibrant and growing in the USA. Some four out of ten Americans belong to a small group, which means an estimated three million groups in the USA, with about 75 million members. Moreover of those who did not currently belong to groups, a high proportion had been involved in a small group in the previous three years. This enlarges the overall picture, suggesting that the majority of adult Americans participate in groups at some stage of their lives. From this Wuthnow argues that the size and spread of these groups is altering American society. He believes that the small-group movement is rooted in the breakdown of traditional support structures and the continuing desire for community. What he calls 'the new quest for community' is

18 Robert Wuthnow, *Sharing the Journey: Support Groups and America's New Quest for Community*, New York and London: Free Press, 1996.

a response to the experience of many Americans 'suffering from isolation, disrupted families, a lack of friends, difficulties in establishing intimate relationships and the demeaning anonymity of large-scale institutions'[19] that are a consequence of the breakdown of neighbourhood and kin structures. At the same time a major feature of the movement is connected to faith. While not all the small groups surveyed were religious or church-connected, the majority were, and among the reasons people were involved was the desire to become more spiritual. This Wuthnow terms 'the search for the sacred', and some of the trends associated with the desire for spirituality might be welcome news to church leaders.

Other findings, however, point to conclusions that would not necessarily have been expected or welcomed by church leaders. In the first place small groups – including Bible-study groups – may not necessarily lead to better Bible knowledge. Neither do they assert the value of denominational traditions nor engage in theological arguments over truth claims. They are more occupied with the group members themselves, promoting mutual help, empathy and encouragement. Much good comes out of these groups – for example, addictions conquered, significance and self-worth gained – but the kind of community fostered is different from the forms that have been lost in family and local community. The core of the small group's life is mutual help without deep challenge, and the God at the heart of the small Christian groups is a God of comfort, support, love and security.

Second, there is within many small groups a highlighting rather than a challenging of individualism. While ostensibly fostering community, the reality is that 'small groups merely provide occasions for individuals to focus on themselves in the presence of others'.[20]

Third, the hopes for the firming up of traditional moral values through small groups are not borne out. Indeed, small groups may make it easier to undermine or cope with the breakdown of these values. For example, belonging to a small group may enable an individual to cope with divorce and the associated transitions

19 Wuthnow, *Sharing the Journey*, p. 12.
20 Wuthnow, *Sharing the Journey*, p. 6.

of marriage break-up that would be much harder without this community of support.

Finally, the yearning for spirituality, often the driving force of the small-group movement, is not stemming the tide of secularity as some claim; rather, secular values may be infiltrating members' thought forms and lifestyles via the small group. Articles of belief that in an earlier time were foundational (such as sin, hell and exclusive salvation for Christians), together with some previously identifiably Christian moral positions and lifestyles, are less central to the small groups surveyed; rather, the meetings provide a place where doubts about certain truth claims may be strengthened by the group's corporate lack of attention to these items, and thus gently laid to one side, and where moral crises and dilemmas can be navigated with the help and support of others without a sense of betraying one's Christian commitment. This 'secularization from within' is what Wuthnow sees as the most worrying.

Small groups are, according to these findings, playing a major role in adapting American religion to the main currents of secular culture at the end of the twentieth century. People have progressively invested less in large-scale institutions and this, Wuthnow argues, will continue. Likewise, church or faith identity will not be taken from large-scale institutions and will be seen to have no special hold over the search for the sacred. In all cases people will look to small groups for coping, learning and support and in order to search for the sacred. The expansion of small groups in the current period may have much to do with their huge advantages for adapting to the fluid social environment. They require little by way of resources other than the commitment of members. They are 'small, relatively fluid, low budget' and 'have an adaptive advantage in a heterogeneous environment such as the contemporary United States'.[21] Thus he concludes that 'if small groups are the glue holding together American society (as some argue), they are then a social solvent as well. They provide a way out of traditional attachments that formerly bound people tightly to their communities.'[22]

---

21 Wuthnow, *Sharing the Journey*, p. 23.
22 Wuthnow, *Sharing the Journey*, p. 25.

My own research in the north-east of England confirms many of Wuthnow's findings. Though the breakdown of local community there is not as extensive as in the USA or elsewhere in the UK, those who are involved in church small groups desire an experience of community, and value most the pastoral support they receive through the friendship and surrogate family they find in their groups. Repeated attempts at making small groups a means of evangelism have failed, even in the most evangelical of churches, and resulting interest in local issues or concerns about justice are low. Within what are essentially mutual support groups there is a genuine desire and enterprise to deepen spirituality, but in a personal and sometimes privatized way.

The history of small groups outlined in the last chapter is important here. The shift in patterns from personal education, self-improvement and social transformation that were hallmarks of church small groups at the beginning of the twentieth century have been replaced by the desire for help in coping with changing patterns of life in both Church and society. Likewise the underlying model of the WEA that can be discerned in the 1919 Report and that influenced the pattern of small groups in church has been replaced by the model of the therapeutic mutual help group. The cultural shift and challenges that Wuthnow highlights are real for Christians, perhaps more so in the post-Christendom, postmodern culture that now prevails. People are looking for a means of survival and the ability to cope. The self-help group offers this and supplies the underlying – and often unconscious – template for Christian small groups.

Summary

So what can we conclude from this body of research on small groups? It may be wise to remember that both findings and reflections are indicative and should not be treated as exact science. Nevertheless I think there are a few things we can say about church-related small groups at the beginning of the twenty-first century in the UK.

- Small groups are highly valued by participants. Surveys consistently return highly positive evaluations of the experience.
- Small groups create a sense of community and provide pastoral care. Indeed at this time this may be their greatest strength as it chimes in with the wider needs of society for community and support at a time of rapid change. If a group lacks other tasks and directions it will default to a pastoral model.
- Small groups act as mediating agents in churches:
  - They offer a sense of intimacy in large and/or growing churches.
  - They provide the opportunity for people to deepen their sense of belonging and commitment.
- Small groups have a capacity to help people own and develop faith. Their slight distance from the institution gives a degree of freedom to explore and express belief combined with the authority to work out faith for themselves.
- Small groups tend to replicate the value of the church or other communities to which they belong. Thus they provide ways for people to be socialized into the values and practices of the church but can also be the means of resistance to those values in some contexts.
- Small groups borrow from and are shaped by forces in wider culture:
  - They meet the needs of people for community and friendship.
  - They are influenced by the popular models around in wider culture and particularly by the self-help group model.
- Small groups are not intrinsically missional. They are not, at least in the UK, a major means of outreach, neighbourhood involvement or an avenue to involvement with issues of justice.

All these insights raise questions for churches that wish to establish small-group ministries. This is the subject of the next chapter.

8

Small Groups and
Discipleship Formation

This chapter attempts to bring together the ideas and information explored so far.

We have identified small groups as potentially playing a role in Christian education. In Chapter 5 we outlined the ways small groups have been used for a variety of purposes. In Chapter 6 we described the history of small groups in the Church in the twentieth century, and in Chapter 7 we related the main lines of recent research on Christian small groups. It is now time to assess the role of small groups in discipleship formation, explore the limitations of this instrument and suggest a practical way for optimizing their use.

To do this we need to remind ourselves of our foundational conviction that the primary means of Christian formation are mission, worship and Christian community. Disciples are formed as they engage in mission in the life of the world, discerning and responding to God's kingdom; as they participate in the worshipping life of God's people; as they live in Christian community. There is no such thing as discipleship formation separated from these. Thus if small groups are to be a useful means of Christian education they must be located within a commitment to mission, worship and community and their relationship must be real and dynamic. Whatever the aim, content or pattern of a small group, if it is to play a part in discipleship formation it must relate to these primary forming energies.

There are some things small groups appear to be good and effective at doing, others they struggle to do well, especially within certain contexts and cultural settings. Some realism is necessary so we do not slip into the formulaic idea that they are the answer, whatever the ills of our Church or nation. It appears that small groups are 'A*' at creating supportive, pastorally caring cultures for their members. Generally, though, they fail to be a means of outreach or a force for promoting justice.

Michael Henderson's book *A Model for Making Disciples* is an analysis of the effectiveness of John Wesley's small-group meetings.[1] In it he makes two significant arguments. The first is that Wesley drew from many sources and tried various experiments before discovering the effective use of small groups for his context. He borrowed from the Moravians, the Anglican societies and Gaston de Renty's small-group experiment, and he worked via trial-and-error to establish societies, classes and bands that were transformational. Second, Wesley was clear what he wanted his system to do. It was to promote scriptural holiness and enable people to make the journey of discipleship together. In doing this he knew where the groups were located in relation to mission and worship. Class and band meetings were not substitutes for worship – converts and members were to worship in the parish church on Sunday. Nor was the small group a primary means of evangelism, though many class members became natural evangelists, and Societies were organized to care for the needy and minister to the poor. If anything, the Society was a form of intentional Christian community, and its small-group-based Christian education was to provide instruction, change behaviour and form affections, within an assumed ongoing commitment to meet God in worship and everyday life.

Our context and John Wesley's are different. This ought to be a warning to those of us who wish to use small groups for our own and others' formation within our church's life. Valuable though a study of Wesley's small groups is, it is unlikely to provide an off-the-shelf model for our own generation. It can, however, serve to inspire and prompt us to examine our situation and experiment

---

1 D. Michael Henderson, *A Model for Making Disciples: John Wesley's Class Meeting*, Nappanee, IN: Evangel Publishing House, 1997.

thoughtfully with small groups to aid and support discipleship formation.

A process for using small groups

Here is a fivefold cyclical process for starting, developing and working with a small-group ministry. It is sequential, but if followed it will lead back again to the beginning in a spiral pattern, hopefully refining and developing the work over time.

Deciding what small groups are for

The first and key question to ask is: What are the groups for? You could answer this in terms of the group activities and experience, but it is probably better answered in terms of outcomes. If the small groups are successful, what would you expect to see?

In the three case studies of the Leech research I conducted (see Introduction), the answers were very different in each church. In one the desired outcomes were that people have a greater sense of belonging to and involvement in the worship life of the parish; that lay and team leadership develop; that a strong sense of being a community grow up with its focus in the Eucharist. In another the desired outcomes were that members find a place in a growing church, build friendships and enter into the church's missional and charismatic ethos. The third wanted to establish Christian presence, worship and outreach across a rural area independent of church buildings. Each had a vision of what the outcomes would be and each chose small groups to achieve it.

How one develops a small-group programme flows from answering the first question: What are the groups for? One church in the North-East was convinced that biblical literacy was the main need of the church and those who joined it. Thus they put their energies into a Disciple course for the whole church, setting a goal of five years for everyone in the church to have followed this 34-week personal and small-group Bible-study programme. They chose this material because it took people through a large proportion of the Bible and at the same time asked them to relate this to their personal discipleship. The hope was that members would come to see this as a rite of passage – a form of catechumenate – and that all new members would in due course be enrolled in an ongoing programme. The church leaders felt they could trust their follow-on small groups to develop in their own ways because all members would by then have a knowledge of the Scriptures and would have been grounded in relating the Bible to personal experience and lifestyle. They recognized that personal friendship and pastoral care would accompany the small-group experience but did not initiate it for that reason. Their vision was a community of biblically literate, self-conscious disciples. The small groups were designed to help them achieve this.

Another way of speaking of outcomes is to identify *values* the church wishes to be at the heart of any expression of Christian faith or church. This has been a key contribution of Cell UK. In identifying their five core values they set out a vision of a small group that reflected the kind of church they and many people were seeking to develop (see p. 99). Phil Potter's version of this puts it in an ABC form:

All involved – every member ministry;
Becoming Disciples – each person active in seeking to grow as a Christian;
Creating Community – making friends and supporting one another in truth and love;
Doing Evangelism – witnessing and inviting others to become disciples;
Encountering God – seeking God in every part of life.[2]

Whether or not you share this vision for church and small group it provides the outcomes that are intended and at the same time indicates the ways the groups are to operate. It can also be an audit tool for personal and group review.

---

2 Phil Potter, *The Challenge of Cell Church: Getting to Grips with Cell Church Values*, Oxford: Bible Reading Fellowship, 2001.

The Anglican parish I studied in 2011 focused its attention on small groups that met for a relatively short time. Their preferred style was a more seasonal use of groups often lasting four to eight weeks. During Lent these took the shape of ecumenical or parish-based study groups. At other times opportunities were provided for those new to the church to help them find their bearings; to those involved in teams preparing the Sunday evening worship during Advent; to confirmation classes that run from Easter onwards. In addition there were six core groups designed to animate and enable church life and growth. These were not perceived of as traditional committees or even task groups as they might be in other churches, rather as ginger groups to stimulate, consult and monitor various aspects of church life, individual members having specific areas of responsibility. All this was carried from the conviction that small-group working allows corporate spirituality to grow in and through the creative and active engagement with the lived life of the church. Newcomers to this parish were offered a pathway through a series of small groups over an 18-month period, designed to embed them in their community's life and worship, and also encouraged to be part of worship teams and small-group ways of developing the life of the church. This approach held clear values of developing lay ministry, teamwork, shared leadership, building community and focusing life in the celebration of Holy Communion. It was what they wanted to achieve, and the ways they wanted to achieve were paved through their use of small groups.

Establishing what small groups are for in any context is the crucial step for their effectiveness. Not only does this help decide on the form, structure and leadership, it also means that one can make use of the natural strengths of small groups and channel more energies towards areas that might be weaker and need more direction. It also allows one to decide what the groups are *not* doing and therefore what parts of the Christian education agenda might be tackled through other means.

This step is a matter of discernment and ought to be pursued:

- *within the framework of the mission of the church.* Most churches have a mission statement or mission slogan that expresses in simple terms how they see their identity and calling. Hopefully this is known and can be articulated by a significant number of the congregation or at least its leadership. If it is not possible to say how the use of small groups is related to the mission of the church, this is a worrying sign. It suggests that either the mission statement or the small-group plan – or both – should be examined afresh. If not it may lead to a confused and confusing set of aims and activities and risks divorcing discipleship formation from mission.

- *with a clear idea of how it relates to worship.* Some churches set up small groups deliberately to link into worship, with an agenda or study material related to preaching themes, the liturgical year or Sunday lectionary. Others will expect small groups to feed into worship occasionally or on a regular basis. A few years ago a church in London ran a Bible Breakfast, where the small group(s) would meet for an early-morning mid-week meal at which they read and discussed the coming Sunday's readings in preparation for a deeper engagement with the Word at worship. Another church uses one of its house groups to lead a worship service once per quarter. In the Anglican parish mentioned above four small-group teams were formed during Advent to plan and run evening worship. Even where small groups have no formal input to worship, there ought to be some sense of how the worship lives of those who attend are to be related to the group's life. It may be as simple as making space for some reflection on worship, developing a group-based worship life or exploring the language of faith in the group.

- *with an eye to the development of discipleship for individuals.* Some of the most effective small groups are those that combine personal responsibility for spiritual growth with the work of the group. The Disciple course mentioned above asks people to do daily Bible study, make notes and reflect on their own discipleship to feed into the weekly meetings. Some groups are built solely around this notion of using the group structure for individual growth. For example, in Covenant Discipleship groups, members help each other identify what each should do for their spiritual development in terms of 'acts of piety' (public worship and personal devotion) and 'acts of mercy' (such as care for neighbours and support for public justice issues). They then covenant together and meet regularly to check how they are getting on.[3] Even if there is no structural link between individual discipleship and the group's aims and purpose, it is at least worth asking the question: What will the groups do to help individuals take responsibility for their own spiritual growth?

Working through all this takes time and effort. It will need to be explored in leadership settings, such as a leadership team, church council or equivalent group, and preferably more widely. It is worth putting on paper and trying out how you would present it on a website or share it with a group of potential group leaders or members. Aim for simplicity and clarity so that anyone can understand what the groups are for, how they relate to Christian calling and why someone might want to join. None of this need mean everything is fixed and will work like clockwork – you can be sure it will not. Neither will it quench the Spirit who continually stirs things and draws us into the purposes of God, but it is abundantly clear that lack of thought and planning about the use of small groups often leads to unsatisfactory initiatives.

Allocating resources

Jesus said that no one builds a tower without first working out whether the resources are there to complete it (Luke 14.28). It is often argued that small groups require little by way of resources since leaders are voluntary, homes of participants serve as venues – and therefore other sites are not required – and there is rarely paid staff. Materials are relatively low cost and expansion merely

---

3 For a fuller description of covenant discipleship, see David Lowes Watson, *Covenant Discipleship: Christian Formation Through Mutual Accountability*, Eugene, OR: Wipf & Stock, 2002.

requires finding another venue and a welcoming host. This sometimes causes people to underestimate the resources needed. In
addition to the time necessary to discuss and communicate the
purpose of small groups widely and at some length, time must
be given to recruiting, preparing, training and sustaining group
leaders. The amount of time needed rises in direct proportion to
the intentionality of the small-group programme and the degree
of control to be employed by the sponsoring church. Some groups
have little need of formal leadership. Indeed research shows that
a small number of groups will elect their own leaders, and leaders
can emerge in the life of a small group. It may be that the nature
of the gathering and the agenda are such that minimal leadership
can facilitate a good meeting, or because all the participants are
well used to small groups from their employment, that leadership
is light-touch or shared. However, in more complex programmes
or initiatives that are culturally new, the need for the commitment
of time to leadership may be significant.

Smaller churches often begin a small-group programme by a
single instance, where the minister, priest or other paid leader
runs a group with the idea of initiating a number of people into
the way of working, and from this group selecting potential
leaders for future groups. This is no bad strategy as it also sig-
nals commitment and participation by leadership, but the second
and subsequent stages are generally more demanding than initiators anticipate. The continued commitment to the desired values,
practices and standards entails encouragement and mentoring for
leaders, regular meetings for quality assurance, cross-fertilization
and reflection and, over time, ways of feeding, inspiring and
refreshing group leaders. And as we outlined earlier, Christian
education involves reflection for the sake of discernment and
learning. This is not simply learning about what works and what
does not. It must distil learning about the nature of mission, worship and insight into God's presence and prompting. Leaders may
be carrying such insight without knowing it and together may be
able to gather wisdom for the life and work of the church.

One church I worked with introduced a system of house groups
that were successful in attracting a good proportion of the church

congregation and drawing in new members. Year on year they seemed to expand their number of groups and added new leaders. The sustained success of this programme, according to the local minister, was building in from the beginning a once-per-quarter leaders' awayday. The day included worship, conversation, a relaxed shared meal, stimulus form an outside speaker and opportunity to reflect together on what the leaders were learning of God.

Valuing leaders

In some ways the previous story makes this point. If there are going to be group leaders, it pays not only to invest in training and ongoing support but also to raise the status of small-groups leaders. The early Methodists had two categories of people who gave direction to their chapel congregations: the Trustees of the building and the Leaders Meeting. These latter were the class leaders. It was assumed they were best placed to discern the will of God and direct the life of the church, because they were situated at the heart of the communities and its spiritual energy – in the class meetings. Folk aspired to be class leaders and felt honoured to be appointed because they recognized that being trusted with this responsibility was to be seen as having the maturity and commitment to help steer the church's mission and ministry.

I have witnessed the same sense of status in a couple of churches where small groups flourish. In one the training for leaders was never open to volunteers! It was made known that it was happening and existing group leaders were invited to nominate someone from their group in whom they saw leadership potential. Those nominated were told the training was in part a vocational discernment exercise for both the church and the individual and that, at the end, there would be a conversation about whether this was the right ministry for the person. Ultimately the church would decide and appoint. The process was not unlike the selection process for ordinands operated in many denominations, and it signalled the importance of this ministry to members of the church. It also reveals another potential role of the group leader, namely to find new leaders. Interestingly, they did not have a problem finding new leaders.

Of course, some churches wanting to use small groups are a long way from this position. Their problem seems to be finding any suitable volunteer who is not already doing several others jobs in the church's life. To raise the status in this context would be to make less confident members feel the task was way beyond their capability. It would deskill rather than enable. If that is your situation, it may be a comfort to know that larger churches also experience this difficulty. Steve Gladen, the small groups' director of Saddleback Church in California with its 3,500 small groups, confesses that they regularly could not find enough people willing to become leaders for their small groups.[4] As a result they developed their HOST scheme. HOST is a simple acronym for the kind of person they began to look for:

H – have a heart for people;
O – open your place;
S – serve a snack;
T – turn on the DVD.

People who could see this in themselves were invited to host – the word 'leader' was not used at this stage – a group for about six weekly sessions. At the end of this short period they could choose to continue hosting the group and were given leadership training and support, or discontinue and rejoin their own small group. Because content and group activities could be supplied on DVD at least for some time (and there are many programmes that now offer this), they could begin at a lower threshold. However, it is clear from reading the account that the status of group leader is high and the training, support and sustenance offered to move people from host to leader is substantial. The starting point has to be discerned in the locality but the role of group leader needs to be greatly respected. They are playing a key role in the care and cure of souls.

4 Steve Gladen, *Small Groups with Purpose: How to Create Healthy Communities*, Grand Rapids, MI: Baker Books, 2011, p. 160.

Devolving responsibility

It is easy to accuse some of the larger churches with extensive small groups of being controlling. The church – via the minister or leadership team – appoints leaders, establishes the values and purpose of the groups, directs the content and activities and monitors or even polices the health and ongoing life of the groups. All this opens these churches up to an accusation of being control freaks! It is easy to see how the McDonaldization notion can be applied to small-group programmes such as Alpha and cell, especially if employed by churches who insist on holding the reins tightly. Of course, this would be defended by saying – as John Wesley did – that churches are simply following a sense of vision, and after all it is a voluntary organization where people can opt out as well as in! But there is more here to be discussed than the degree to which the church seeks to control the ethos, doctrine and practices of the church members.

If we recognize the organic nature of the kingdom as Jesus portrayed it, we immediately recognize that how things will grow and develop is uncertain and unpredictable. Who knows which seed will fall on stony ground or which on fertile soil? Who sees in advance which small mustard seed will be a huge tree and which will die in the earth? Who can tell which new shoots are wheat and which are tares? And who risks pulling up the weeds and inadvertently uprooting the promise of the kingdom? There is a tension in the life of the church between being faithful (apostolic) and making every effort to maintain the unity of the Spirit, on the one hand, and replicating the trust God places in us by trusting other people to be channels of God's purpose and love, on the other. 'Trust' and 'devolving power and responsibility' are different terms for the same thing.

How much should be devolved to small groups is an important question for churches developing this ministry.

I was deeply challenged by a minister from a small new church in St Albans a couple of years ago. In conversation he told me about his church, as I was interested in the small-group structure they had. They had started the church through a small-group meeting, and small groups had been part of their way of being church from the beginning. Now after 20 years they had about 80 people worshipping on Sunday and slightly more in their mid-week groups. He related that a key decision of the leadership was to cease to make mission initiatives as a whole church and to ask each group to discern and decide mission initiatives they felt they could take. Mission was understood broadly. One group said it wanted to put on a Christian rock concert outreach event; another decided to get involved with the homeless; another to partner a charity working in Sudan; another to do something for the local environment through cleaning up streets, removing graffiti and repainting a playground. While this was exciting and seemed to confirm that the decision of the leadership had been a good one, it altered the nature of his ministry. This man was experienced at preaching and leading churches. He had seen his job as discerning vision and persuading the church to take up the challenge and get involved. This had suddenly changed. Instead of trying to discern the vision and enthuse others, he now found himself working as a mentor to the small groups. He confessed that some of the ideas were 'off the wall' but he had come to see his role not as the authority to permit or prevent certain actions – though of course he alerted people to the pitfalls and challenges – but to encourage and enable, and to trust that the groups should takes the risks and learn from mistakes, as well as delight in the fruit.

The encounter made me realize that finding the right balance between clear aims and outcomes for small groups, and encouraging appropriate responsibility and initiative to lie with the groups, is hard. My view is that at present we either have no clear sense of what our small groups are for or, if we have, we err on the side of church direction and control. I wonder if, when our aims, outcomes and values are as clear as they can be, more should be devolved to small groups so that a wider number of folk can be involved in discerning the mind of the Spirit. Democracy may not be the order of the kingdom but the 'sense of the faithful' might be better grasped if people were to take initiatives and risks within a supporting framework.

Reviewing and developing

The term 'reviewing' sounds very much like control and the worst kind of scrutiny. It echoes the business model of dispensing with the failing and building on the successful (usually measured in terms of profitability). Here reviewing means something slightly different. It involves asking questions about whether what we hoped and aimed for is being realized; whether the kingdom values we have sought to pursue are becoming visible; whether there are surprises and developments we had not anticipated from which God wants us to learn.

This is where outcomes in terms of kingdom values are most helpful. Saddleback Church, which we mentioned above, builds its whole church life around what it calls the five New Testament purposes of the Church. This set of purposes, drawn from Acts 2.42–7, is identified as (a) fellowship; (b) growing as disciples; (c) ministering to each other; (d) evangelizing the lost; (e) worship. There might be some discussion about the exegesis of this passage and what weight these five verses should carry for a full ecclesiology, but as a set of values or outcomes for small groups and personal development as disciples, they serve as a useful structure. Clearly they are mission- and worship-related – though mission has a limited focus – and there is the implicit idea that growth into Christlikeness will be an active process in a number of areas. They use the set as a form of checklist for three levels of reflection: the individual Christian; the small group; the church as a whole. In each zone the question is posed: Is there movement and growth here and what signs indicate growth? The five purposes are used as a template for individual growth and to audit the group's life, not so much to commend or condemn but see where the balance lies and what might need to be attended to more in future.

The main point here is not the particular values that are advocated in this scheme but the practice of reflection and review of the aims and values that were envisaged.

It is widely acknowledged that John Wesley's much-admired class meetings started for a purpose different from the one for which they became famous. Originating as a scheme for collecting money to pay off the loan on the Bristol Building (a penny a week from each member of the 12 members of a subdivision of the Society), they rapidly became the engine of Methodist spirituality. Wesley already had small groups running in his societies that were called bands, but they were not as popular as he had hoped and did not do what he most needed them to do with the growing numbers coming to faith from among the poor, where drunkenness, violence and what he considered to be unethical ways of survival – such as smuggling – were part of the context and a constant temptation. Wesley recognized quite quickly that the class meeting, with its class leader in touch with each member each week, was an effective form of both pastoral support and oversight. When this developed into a weekly meeting where members shared their experience of living the Christian life, their temptations, triumphs and failures, and challenged one another's behaviour, it had become a means of transformation. Henderson describes this as spiritual education in the 'behavioural mode', meaning it aimed at and was effective in changing behaviours.[5] The genius of John Wesley was to recognize this quickly, utilize classes for kingdom purposes and help what Skinner calls the 'half converted'[6] to make progress on the road to holiness.

Randy Frazee, in his book *The Connecting Church*, tells the story of the rebuilding of a congregation, having lost two-thirds of its membership in the period prior to 1990. The building up of the congregation involved the extensive use of small groups, but after considerable growth the staff team found themselves reviewing their small-group programme almost by accident.

Before we began our opening session, somewhere in the room a conversation broke out. The topic was personal small group satisfaction. Someone on our staff had the audacity to confess that the small group experience was unsatisfying. Once the virus was airborne it spread like the black plague. One staff member after the other shared their disappointment. Now, if

---

5 Henderson, *A Model for Making Disciples*, pp. 93ff.

6 M. Skinner, *House Groups*, London: Epworth Press, 1969; see esp. appendix A.

the corporate dissatisfaction had been aimed at proper lumbar support in our office chairs, that would have been one thing. However, we were confessing that our central vehicle for assimilation and spiritual growth wasn't working for the most motivated members of our church. I, too, shared my discontent. The agenda quickly changed. We spent the entire day talking openly about the best-kept secret in our church: small groups were not achieving authentic community.[7]

The rest of the book is a description of how the church sought to deepen its understanding of community and developed its small groups in new ways with different and more demanding values. Frazee recognizes what Robert Wuthnow has described: small groups that heighten individualism and move people away from engagement with their neighbours and neighbourhoods. The review that began on the day of the staff meeting led to a development of small groups that had a more authentic expression of community and a stronger relationship to the localities and all the issues faced by local residents.

This is a story of reviewing and developing small groups and identifying a deep flaw that needed addressing.

The fivefold process of developing small groups that I have laid out in this chapter, is not meant to be exhaustive – there are other ways of conceiving the process of small-group ministry development. The approach does not advocate one way of using small groups but encourages a methodical approach in the light of the information and insight gained from research and the wisdom within the Church and wider society. It is offered for those who want to embark or develop this ministry to help discipleship formation. The next and final chapter will offer some theological reflection on small-group ministry.

---

7 Randy Frazee, *The Connecting Church: Beyond Small Groups to Authentic Community*, Grand Rapids, MI: Zondervan, 2001, p. 20.

9

Disciples Together:
Small Groups in Theological
Perspective

God is the creator of all human beings, with their difference, their colours, their races, their religions. Be attentive: Every time you draw nearer to your neighbour, you draw nearer to God. Be attentive: Every time you go further from your neighbour, you go further from God.[1]

Those who write about small groups in the church often give very little attention to a theological rationale for the enterprise, being more concerned about the practicalities of setting up and running successful programmes. There is much to be said for this neglect. First, it implicitly recognizes the neutrality of small groups. They are widespread, naturally occurring as well as deliberately constructed phenomena, present in families, workplaces, leisure and educational endeavours. Small groups did not begin in the New Testament Church and there is nothing unique in the Christian use of small groups save perhaps the purposes to which they are put and the world view in which they are held. Second, there is no appeal to biblical, ecclesiastical or divine authority to impose certain structures or approaches. These writers are content that the advice and agenda they offer does not need a divine imprimatur

---

1 A sign in Arabic in the Elias Chacour library in Ibillin near Haifa. This translation is taken from Thomas G. Kirkpatrick, *Small Groups in the Church: A Handbook for Creating Community*, Bethesda, MD: The Alban Institute, 1995, p. 15.

to be practically useful. Finally, it avoids what Emmanuel Lartey calls 'scavenging' for theology; that is, where having done work in other disciplines such as sociology and having found practical solutions for some issue, a writer then searches around for some biblical or theological gloss when in fact the contribution is already made from the other sources.

On the other hand, small groups are a recurring part of church life. This in itself is worthy of attention and theological reflection. Moreover in our own time, as some churches are tending towards an ecclesiology that assumes small-group membership, it is becoming more pressing to explore the role of these groups in theological as well as sociological terms.

Three theological views of small groups

When small groups are justified in theological terms, broadly there are three lines of theological assertion.

- The small group is church.
- Small groups represent *ekklesiolae in ekklesia* – a source of renewal for the church.
- Small groups are a special expression of *koinonia*.

We will consider each in turn.

The small group is church

The argument here is that the New Testament churches were in effect small groups and represent a primitive and pure ecclesial form.[2] A key text is Acts 5.42, which says that the first post-Pentecost Christians met in the Temple and in 'private homes'.

---

2 See, for example, Ron Trudinger, *Cells for Life: Home Groups – God's Strategy for Church Growth*, Eastbourne: Kingsway, 1983. This idea that small groups are a New Testament pattern is asserted throughout the book, but see chapter 3 for the basis of the argument. See also David Prior, *The Church in the Home*, Basingstoke: Marshall Pickering, 1983, p. 7.

These meetings of the church in homes are noted on several occasions in the New Testament either directly (Acts 12.12) or indirectly, in the way Paul refers to the church in the homes of named individuals (Rom. 16.14f.; 1 Cor. 1.16; Col. 4.15; Philemon 1.2). The closure or unreceptiveness of the synagogue to the Christian message (Acts 19) and the absence of church buildings for at least 150 years suggest that this house-based form was the norm for the Early Church and, as New Testament writings are addressed to churches who met in this form, the assumed ecclesiology is that of the small group.

There is certainly sufficient material in Paul's letters to show that modern small groups have much in common with these Early Church gatherings. As Wayne Meeks writes:

> These letters [of Paul] also reveal that those groups enjoyed an unusual degree of intimacy, high levels of interaction among members, and a very strong sense of internal cohesion and of distinction both from outsiders and from the 'world'.[3]

There are, however, a number of problems with making an equation that identifies the small group as the ideal or primal form of church.

First, our knowledge about the nature of the earliest churches is sketchy and much debated. That they met in homes is not disputed; what kind of homes they met in is less clear. Scholars have tended to conceive of believers meeting in a traditional Roman *domus* (house) with *triclinium* (dining room) and *atrium* (courtyard) provided by a wealthy member of the congregation.[4] This would have afforded a potential meeting space for 40–50 people. If this is true and typical, in terms of size, it is more like a small

3 Wayne A. Meeks, *The First Uban Christians: The Social World of the Apostle Paul*, 2nd edn, New Haven and London: Yale University Press, 2003, p. 74.

4 Edward Adams, 'First-Century Models for Paul's Churches: Selected Scholarly Developments since Meeks', in Todd D. Still and David G. Horrell (eds), *After the First Urban Christians: The Social-scientific Study of Pauline Christianity Twenty-five Years Later*, London and New York: T. & T. Clark, 2009, p. 65.

congregation than a small group. The idea has been challenged by Justin Meggitt, who contends that as 97 per cent of the population of the Roman Empire lived in abject poverty, Christians would not have had access to the kind of *domus* most have imagined.[5] Excavations at Pompeii, however, reveal a wide range of size of apartments within buildings and have tended to reinforce that gatherings could easily have been 40-plus in the home of, for example, a master cabinet maker. Robert Banks has argued that some poorer traders would have no meeting space but would engage in fellowship while at their craft (perhaps 'Chloe's people' in 1 Cor. 1.11), but generally he concurs with the majority that some households were offered and used for gatherings of 20–50.[6]

If size indicates one difference from modern small groups, other features of the Early Church *oikos* would have been equally alien. In the first century the 'household' was larger and more diverse than modern notions of family home. In addition to relatives it might include slaves, freedmen, hired workers and tenants or partners in trade or craft. Buildings were often divided up, with sections reserved for members according to gender or status.[7] Relationships would have structured along hierarchical lines, with the head having some legal responsibility for the household and an expectation that the acceptance of superior and inferior roles in it were essential to the right ordering of society. Some might have been compelled to be present at church gatherings. Roger Gehring discusses the effects of this structure for mission[8] and Carolyn Osiek points out that meetings set within such social and physical architecture perpetuated the disadvantages

5 Justin J. Meggitt, *Paul, Poverty and Survival*, Studies of the New Testament and Its World, Edinburgh: T. & T. Clark, 1998.

6 Peter Oakes, *Reading Romans in Pompeii: Paul's Letter at Ground Level*, London: SPCK, 2009. The idea that this was typical of the Empire now has the support of most scholars. See Adams, 'First-Century Models for Paul's Churches', p. 67; Robert J. Banks, *Paul's Idea of Community: The Early House Churches in their Historical Setting*, Exeter: Paternoster Press, 1980.

7 Carolyn Osiek and David L. Balch, *Families in the New Testament World: Households and House Churches*, Louisville, KY.: Westminster John Knox Press, 1997.

8 Roger W. Gehring, *House Church and Mission: The Importance of Household Structures in Early Christianity*, Peabody, MA: Hendrickson, 2004.

of women, slaves and social inferiors.[9] While it may be argued that the impact of the gospel would transform such social ordering, there is evidence that tensions arose precisely because of the particular social dynamics of these household gatherings. All in all these are not best read as front-room small-group fellowships but as a distinctive pattern of medium-sized communities in the first-century Roman world.

Even if the church did meet in groups of fewer than 20 members in places, this does not necessarily mean it is to be taken as normative for the Church. The New Testament bears witness to diverse understandings of the Church[10] and ever-changing and developing forms of gathering and worship. The use of buildings went through at least three phases before the Constantinian Basilicas – the house church, the church house and the church hall – while different ecclesiologies developed alongside changing patterns of church organization and structure.

Finally, the classical marks of ecclesiology do not sit easily with the modern pattern of small groups. The signs or notes of the Church expressed in the Creeds as 'one, holy, catholic and apostolic' imply something larger than the solitary group. That is not to say that these hallmarks, which are both the gift of God and the calling of God's people, cannot be manifest in small groups. This very setting may be the occasion of encounter with God's holiness or the sense of unity with others that comes through grace, but the notions of catholicity and apostolicity imply connectedness across both time and space that would at least require a network or sense of belonging to other groups and church forms. Likewise the Reformation idea of the Church being the place where the Word of God is truly preached and the sacraments duly administered does not fit with the reality of small groups. While a small number of churches devolve sacraments to their small groups, the vast majority of such groups contain neither preaching nor the celebrations of baptism and Holy Communion. It is empirically rare for small groups to desire or claim these – the focus of

9 Osiek and Balch, *Families in the New Testament World*, p. 221.

10 James D. G. Dunn, *Unity and Diversity in the New Testament: An Inquiry into the Character of Earliest Christianity*, London: SCM Press, 1977.

their activity is elsewhere. More basic concepts such as 'wherever people join together to respond to Christ as Lord – there is the Church'[11] may well work for a small-group ecclesiology, but recent reflections on fresh expressions of church that often begin in small-group form have often seen these as on their way to being church and have tended to raise the number of marks identifying the church.[12] On none of these measures does the small group seem adequate of itself to be identified as church. While it is possible for small groups to experience and carry much of what it means to be church, on the whole the identification of small groups with being church is neither secure nor useful.

Small groups as ekklesiolae in ekklesia

Some have argued that small groups are pockets or sources of renewal necessary for the continual reformation of the Church. The phrase *ekklesiolae in ekklesia* (little churches within the Church) was first articulated in the seventeenth century by Philip Jacob Spener, but to understand it we must trace its emergence in the wake of the Reformation.

Peter Bunton traces the beginning of church-related small groups in their modern form back to the Reformation.[13] Luther is credited with creating the climate for and possibility of small Christian groups meetings by his arguing for the priesthood of all believers – meaning that believers might minister to one another – and by outlining three forms of church in his Preface to the German Mass: the Latin Mass; the vernacular (German) Mass; those who assemble themselves in 'some house ... to pray, read, baptize and receive the sacrament and practise other Christian works'. When added to the desire of translators such as William Tyndale to put the Bible 'into the hands of the common ploughboy'

---

11 Methodist Church, *Called to Love and Praise*, Peterborough: Methodist Publishing House, 1999. 2.4.9.

12 Anglican–Methodist Working Party, 'Fresh Expressions in the Mission of the Church', London: Church House Publishing, 2012.

13 Peter Bunton, *Cell Groups and House Churches: What History Teaches Us*, Ephrata, PA: House to House Publications, 2001.

the Reformation gives a strong impetus to small-group gatherings. In reality Luther never implemented small-group or house-church meetings, claiming that believers were not ready for them; rather, small groups sprang up in the radical reformation movement encouraged by Zwingli around 1520 – initially for teaching and then for survival for the persecuted. The civic authorities banned small-groups meetings in Zurich in 1525, thus forcing Anabaptist and other groups secretly into homes.

From this period onwards, small groups sprang up in various places, primarily in Protestant communities, but because they were always accompanied by a possibility of schism and separation from the national Church, there were regular prohibitions on such gatherings. This placed many advocates in a difficult position, desiring the more intense piety that could grow in a small group to renew the Church but fearing the separation that might result. Philip Jacob Spener attempted to solve the dilemma by developing the notion of *ekklesiolae in ekklesia*. Small groups could and should be convened for unity and closer fellowship, he argued, but they should be open only to members of the church and strictly under the oversight of the church minister. In other words, small groups only had meaning within the larger frame of the Church and were intended to provide a nucleus of believers with the object that they 'might leaven and influence the life of the whole church for the better'.[14] This idea seems to underpin the Religious Societies of the seventeenth century in England, founded by the Revd Dr Horneck, a German Lutheran who became Anglican and whose societies were open only to those who were members of the Church of England.

One might argue that within the Roman Catholic Church the religious orders provide the same role of being vehicles of the Spirit for the renewal of the Church, while holding their members within the larger body of the Church. From such figures as Francis of Assisi and Ignatius Loyola the energy for the purifying

---

14 Martyn Lloyd-Jones, '*Ecclesiola in Ecclesia*', available at www.the-highway.com/ecclesia_Lloyd-Jones.html. It is also found in David Martyn Lloyd-Jones, *The Puritans: Their Origins and Successors*, London: Banner of Truth Trust, 1987.

and renewing of the Church has often grown in religious communities, whose rules of life sought to embody some essentials of the gospel. These could also be described as *ekklesiolae in ekklesia.*

The renewalist strand in the notion was no doubt attractive to John Wesley, who defended his societies, classes and lay preachers as channels for the renewal the Church of England – expedient and temporary. Yet he did not restrict membership of his societies to Anglicans and thus he risked separation from the beginning. As Martyn Lloyd-Jones pointed out, the Wesleys, along with others in the Evangelical Revival, had another need, namely what to do with new converts who were ill at ease in the parish church and often only half converted.[15] Thus while John Wesley embraced *ekklesiolae in ekklesia* theoretically, in practice he began to develop a small-group form of catechumenate with its eyes on practical holiness.

While *ekklesiolae in ekklesia* retains its appeal as a source of renewal,[16] the idea is judged to be unscriptural and to be doomed to failure by those who have desired a more radical recovery of 'true Church' by falling to the lowest common denominator rather than leavening the whole.[17] On a broader front it no longer fits the empirical reality of most small groups in churches. Even in the Network or Restorationist churches, many of which began as small groups seeking a pure church, small groups are now seen as more of a 'keep net' for nurturing Christian disciples rather than a fishing rod for outreach or a purifying agent for the life of the Church.

Small groups are a special expression of koinonia

As small groups in a variety of spheres have a proven track record of creating or deepening a sense of community, it is perhaps not surprising that the word often used in the New Testament to name

---

15 Lloyd-Jones, *The Puritans*, p. 10.

16 For example, see Steven J. L. Croft, *Transforming Communities: Re-Imagining the Church for the 21st Century*, London: Darton, Longman & Todd, 2002, p. 72.

17 Lloyd-Jones, *The Puritans*.

Christian community is brought into theological reflection on small groups.[18] *Koinonia* appears over 20 times in the New Testament. It has a range of meanings, from association, communion and fellowship, through generosity and gift to participation and sharing. Its use in Acts 2.42 to describe the experience of the first Christian community and its regular appearance in Paul's comments about the Church, together with its special connection to Holy Communion (1 Cor. 10.16),[19] identifies it as a key biblical word.

Much has been written about *koinonia* in recent years, especially in ecumenical theology, and it has often been linked with the nature of the Trinity. Just as the Trinity is regularly portrayed as the mutual indwelling of the persons of the Trinity, so *koinonia* is an experience in the church of the divine community. When the Church receives the gift of God, experiencing and expressing its diversity as a rich unity of interdependent persons, it is touching and echoing the life of God. When this is manifest in the Church it is to be taken as a sign or reflection of the Triune God.

Many, for good reason, would claim that their experience of small groups takes them to a deeper and more satisfying experience of human community, one that resonates and relates to the very life of God. It is interesting to note that the most common translation of *koinonia*, as 'fellowship', was far and away the word used most often to identify what was central and best about small groups, according to the Leech research. Robert Wuthnow also highlighted the centrality of the quest for community in small groups, and the stories from case studies regularly identify community as the source of both strength and renewal for individual members.

Without denying the experience of group members, nor the ability of small groups to open up a depth of sharing and mutual support, this high claim is one that cannot be uniquely confined to the small-group context. There are many testimonies to the transcending unity encountered in preaching, prayer, the intimate

---

18 See for example, Kirkpatrick, *Small Groups in the Church*, p. 5.

19 The cup of thanksgiving is described as participation (*koinonia*) in Christ – see 1 Cor. 10.16ff.

moments of Holy Communion and in encounter with the vulnerable and needy. Just as *koinonia* is a larger and richer concept in the New Testament than the coming together of Christians to meet and study, so the life of God when seen and experienced in the Church is likely to break in in a variety of forms and places. That *koinonia* can be experienced in small-group meetings of Christians must be affirmed, but it is hardly an exclusive identifier.

In search of a theological perspective

None of these three ways of speaking about small groups theologically offers an adequate or comprehensive understanding, fitting both the empirical experience and ecclesiological context. Each captures some aspect of the small-group experience in the church, or perhaps it is better to say that because small groups serve a variety of functions in the life of the church, these descriptors touch on small groups in different modes or about different tasks. In the early stage of new church movements the small group often serves as the embryonic church, holding in its life the DNA of the new emerging church; at times of significant change or ecclesial stagnation, small groups can provide the energy to challenge and renew the wider Church and to grow new ways of expressing the good news; and for some small groups there are moments of intense, intimate mutuality in community that are windows into the life and character of God – sometimes felt when this is not as evident in wider church life.

It is tempting to accept that small groups do not need separate theological status or justification. It may be better to acknowledge that some objects and social constructions only have a theological significance in the use to which they are put.

This seems, however, too little for this recurring and currently growing phenomenon. Hence I will sketch another way of thinking about small groups. In this sketch, rather than begin with small groups, I reflect on the theological significance of companionship and then turn to consider the nature of the Church as a pilgrim people.

Companions in the way

The Walk to Emmaus (Luke 24) tells a beautiful story of revelation, hope and transformation. This is not a small group in any conventional sense; rather, it is two people who journey together, and the fact that they stay in the same house has given some commentators to believe that they may well have been husband and a wife or close relatives. Whatever the relation to each other, for the seven-mile journey from Jerusalem to Emmaus[20] they are companions, accompanying one another at a time of sadness and the brokenness of their hopes. They walk side by side, quite slowly one imagines, as they make this homeward journey. They are in danger of being overwhelmed by what has happened in Jerusalem, and it is only when they sense another alongside them that things begin to change. The Scriptures come to life, their hearts burn within them, their conversation is expanded, their minds stretched; and, no doubt, their pace quickens in the company of this stranger. When their eyes are fully opened, and they see it is Jesus who has been with them, broken the bread and disappeared from their sight, they are filled with new energy and return to the city to tell their story to the other disciples, gathered together and also celebrating the good news of Jesus.

In some ways this is the prototype of the rhythm of discipleship I spoke of earlier in this book. Here we see two people in the midst of the ordinary world – making their way home after the annual Passover festival in Jerusalem and having to face what comes next with heavy hearts, recently robbed of hope. But in this difficult time they encounter Jesus, risen from the dead, a sign of the promised kingdom breaking into their sorrow-filled reality. They have left the community of disciples in Jerusalem, and it is to them they return to tell of their extraordinary experience. There they discover that others have good news too, and their experience is added to the growing sense of joy. They have discovered God in the world and in the assembly, and this will

---

20 The actual length of journey is not known because the original site of Emmaus is not easy to identify, but seven miles seems roughly right for Luke's description and the fact that they made the same journey back after supper.

in turn propel them into other experiences and encounters. The story is an account of transformation, and it models the forming and transforming dynamic of the Church as gathering, dispersing and gathering again.

It is no accident that this parable of transformation is set in the context of companions. These two dispirited disciples are renewed and changed in the company of each other and by the presence of Jesus, as they journey together. Many of the significant moments of transformation in the story of the Early Church are at moments of meeting and accompanying. Notice the unwelcome encounter between Paul and Ananias (Acts 9), where the latter is afraid and naturally wary of the former; and yet God brings them together so that both grow in the faith. In the scattering of Acts 8[21] caused by persecution, Philip travels for a time alongside an Ethiopian eunuch and the good news is shared. A couple of chapters on, Peter is prompted to travel to the house of Cornelius, where to everyone's surprise, including Peter's, God is already at work. Notice that Peter returns to Jerusalem believers and shares his story with them (Acts 11). We could add to this those missionary journeys undertaken by two or three companions. All these stories tell about companions to whom, in whom or with whom Jesus is made known, and set within the gathering and dispersing of God's people.

Companions on a journey is a regular way of telling the Christian story. In my childhood I was introduced to *Pilgrim's Progress*. In John Bunyan's classic story of the journey of faith, the central character, Christian, regularly walks with companions, some of whom want to steer him from the right path and others point him to the true way. These include characters named Evangelist, Worldly Wiseman, Prudence, Demas, Talkative, Faithful and Hopeful. As a young child I imagined these were real people travelling some leg of the journey with him, not symbols of Christian life. When I was a little older I did see the analogies. Now I want to retain the idea that these were real companions who embodied what their names signified, because this resonates with my

---

21 The word used here is *diaspareio*, from which we get the English word 'dispersed'.

spiritual journey. I own much to several small groups on my faith journey, but I owe much more to individuals who have been my companions. Some of these I have met in the course of work or church, others on the way; often people of deep Christian faith, sometimes of faiths other than Christian and occasionally of no professed faith at all. With each I learned something new and was strengthened in my faith. From one I learned something of humility; from another the nature of serving; from another kindness; from another boldness and the willingness to take risks for love's sake. In each case it was as if on the journey we hit on a new depth of humanity characterized by genuine respect, real honesty and an open vulnerability that allowed for change.

Sometimes this sense of enlightenment through companions has been spoken of as holy or spiritual friendship. Ambrose and Augustine of Hippo, those giants of the Early Church, spoke of it, and Aelred of Rievaulx, the twelfth-century British abbot, wrote a book in three parts on the subject.[22] In recent times the notion has been picked up by theologians such Gregory Jones.[23]

Jones summarizes his view of holy friendship as

> What constitutes holy friendships? Holy friends challenge the sins we have come to love, affirm the gifts we are afraid to claim and help us dream dreams we otherwise would not dream.

This seems to encapsulate what might be deemed necessary for transformation, and of course all these writers assume a commitment to the way of faith as the basis on which such robust and releasing friendships can work. The holy dimension is the belief that God is at work forming us on the way, so that companionship may become a facilitating relationship.

In Aelred's third section of his writing he identifies something vital: as he is discussing the practical issues of choosing, test-

---

22 Aelred, *Spiritual Friendship*, ed. Marsha L. Dutton, Collegeville, MN: Liturgical Press, 2010.

23 L. Gregory Jones and Kevin R. Armstrong, *Resurrecting Excellence: Shaping Faithful Christian Ministry*, Grand Rapids, MI: Eerdmans, 2006; see esp. chapter 3.

ing, admitting and enjoying friends (and dissolving friendships), he says that these real, embodied friendships are to be held in an eschatological frame, looking forward to God's final reign where all will exist in friendship. What he means is that particular experiences of holy companionship are foretastes of what God is bringing for all humankind – a friendship that reflects the friendship of God to human beings and wherein we recognize and celebrate that we are all children of God.

This is important, if we are to be saved from thinking that this is some kind of holy huddle with 'folk like us' and thus not enabled to see companionship in its widest sense. Here Elias Chacour's words of wisdom at the beginning of this chapter are a good counterbalance. They remind us that meeting with God is not confined to those who already share our Christian faith. God is in every neighbour, and the imperative is to be attentive and draw close to our neighbours.

> God is the creator of all human beings, with their difference, their colours, their races, their religions. Be attentive: Every time you draw nearer to your neighbour, you draw nearer to God. Be attentive: Every time you go further from your neighbour, you go further from God.

Thus in every companion in this life we have the potential to learn of God.

In this light we can now speak of small groups as regular and recurring features of church life. For small groups represent to us the call to embrace companionship. By our willingness to join and participate in small groups we signal our desire to walk with others on the road to transformation. Recognizing that God forms us through various means in mission, worship and community, joining a small group for a task, for study, personal support or missionary endeavour is a symbolic commitment to being disciples together, living with diversity and open to the growth that may come to us from others – for the sake of the kingdom and our transformation within it. This does not mean everyone needs the companionship provided by a small group. There are many ways of journeying with others, including with those of another or no faith, that are filled with potential for growth. The point is that small groups in our church life remind us that journeying with others different from ourselves is central to Christian faith and needs to be actively taken up. It is a sign and gesture in which we recognize our corporate calling.

Let us now place this idea within a larger frame.

The Church as a pilgrim people

The most helpful image of the Church in which to speak of companionship, discipleship formation and the role of small groups is that of the pilgrim people. Although this term is never used in the Bible, it captures a series of experiences that tell us about the ways God forms God's people. There is a strong sense of pilgrimage in the story of Abraham leaving home and family and travelling in pursuit of God's promise. This, though focused on Abraham, is no individual journey but one made by a small community, with relatives, workers, slaves and herds all moving together. This community would have moved slowly, but the movement is significant for it is through the internal relationships and external encounters on the way that God's purpose is gradually revealed and known. The same sense of growth through journey lies at the heart of the Exodus and the desert wanderings of God's people. They are people on the way, learning to inhabit a new identity. It is echoed in the Psalms of Ascent (Psalms 120–134) that would have been sung as people travelled to Jerusalem for the great festivals and it is reimagined in Isaiah 40 onwards as the prophet envisages a holy road that God's people will travel (from Exile). Jesus would have been familiar with these writings and with the experience of pilgrimage (Luke 2.41). He chose to employ the same means for the fulfilment of his mission and the formation of his company of disciples. The disciples were formed as they journeyed with Jesus.

The New Testament picks up and continues this idea of a people on the move towards the final fulfilment of God's promises. The letter to the Hebrews looks back to the people of faith recounted in Hebrew Scriptures and describes them as aspiring 'to a better country' (Heb. 11.16). This better country the author describes as heavenly – in other words, a home in God to which these great characters and the Christian Church are now travelling together. The citizenship of those who follow Jesus is in heaven (Phil. 3.20; Eph. 2.19) and while this means we are 'no longer strangers and aliens' but fellow citizens with the Jewish people, our existential experience will be that we are not at home yet but on the way (1 Pet. 2.9–12).

The value of this image is that it combines the idea of movement and learning. A people on the move may not travel fast but the journey itself gives rise to opportunities of discovering and knowing more. They learn on the hoof and the learning is concrete, earthy, embodied and relational. The metaphor is also fundamentally eschatological; that is, it is orientated to God's future, towards which we are moving and being drawn. We have a foretaste here and now but the fullness is yet to be. Hence there is always a provisionality and humility about our knowing and a desire to press on to something better, clearer and more whole.

Those who have been on a pilgrimage know there are some common features of the experience. For one thing there is companionship and conversation. Unless you make a pilgrimage in a remote place and on your own, you will most likely walk with someone for a part of the journey. This walking together is sometimes filled with small talk, easy exchange and light banter, sometimes it takes the form of profound sharing and sometimes it consists of walking in silence or a quiet appreciation of company that requires no words to be spoken. Another feature is that of encounter: the meeting of a person or place or object that is new and different, perhaps even challenging, and requires thought and reflection. Then there are times when you are alone – sometimes even in company – when your thoughts, without prompting, bubble up from within and take you to past incidents or current dilemmas that the physical act of walking has somehow released. This may simply be the remembrance or even the sadness of some part of your experience, but it may lead you to explore old things in new ways, provoking fresh insight or resolve.

Pilgrimage is a powerful metaphor in our own age. Witness the popularity of *The Unlikely Pilgrimage of Harold Fry*.[24] Although not ostensibly a religious book, this novel tells the story of a retired man who on the receipt of a letter from a former colleague writes a reply and sets off to post it. He finds he cannot bring himself to post the letter at the nearby postbox and so decides to walk to the next, delaying the moment of letting go, only to find that the same thing happens at the next box. And so, in short, he finds himself walking from the south coast of England to Berwick in the north to deliver the message in person. The story is then a series of encounters, companions and conversations, with much time spent reviewing his life, experience and relationships. Suffice to say that the journey is both revelatory and healing and there are even a few moments of transcendence. It is a form of *Pilgrim's Progress* for a twenty-first-century secular society. Its appeal is surely in part the sense of personal growth and new insight made possible through movement and encounter. It speaks to people's life experience, perhaps particularly in a postmodern age with its individual sense of journey.

The Church can lay claim to a permanent pilgrimage and, further, that this pilgrimage names God as the one who invites us to and is the goal of ours. It is God who also enables the journey by his grace and truth made continually known in Jesus. The pilgrim people of God are journeying towards God's kingdom and being formed by its king.

Thus it is here that we can locate discipleship formation. As we have argued earlier, disciples are actively formed as they participate in the mission of God in the life of the world, as they worship and wonder at the God revealed in Jesus and as they live intentionally in Christian community. Disciples live a rhythm of gathering and dispersing, sent into the world as agents and partners of a loving God and gathered together for praise, prayer and reflection. This is a dynamic movement, a continuous dance of faith, in which disciples repeatedly meet with the risen Christ to be challenged and changed by him, to be made like him and to

24 Rachel Joyce, *The Unlikely Pilgrimage of Harold Fry*, London: Doubleday, 2012.

delight in the signs of God's presence. Those precious moments of reflection and recognition that grace makes possible and in which God is glimpsed, serve to shape, strengthen and sustain the energy and resolve for taking the next steps and keeping in tune with the music. But this regular rhythm of faith takes place within the larger movement of a pilgrim people whose compass is on God's kingdom and whose calling is to God's future. Like the earth spinning on its axis, while at the same time orbiting the sun, so the forming of God's people and its individual members takes place within two different but interlocking movements.

It is here we can also locate small groups. Small groups in the life of the Church represent in microcosm the calling to be a pilgrim people. In meeting and working with a discrete collection of individuals, members are afforded the possibilities of travelling with others for a short time with all the potential this holds. Because by its very creation in the life of the Church it acknowledges the companionship of the risen Christ, any small group can lead to deeper knowledge of ourselves, others and God. A small group can also be a dojo (see p. 63) for Christian practices of care, respect, the nurturing of the gifts of others, the distilling of insights, the opportunity to be truthful and accountable and to give and receive forgiveness. These practices are the essence of authentic Christian community. Above all the small group offers the possibility of encounter with difference through which God often speaks and God holds in mysterious unity. It does not matter what the small group is for or how long it meets – each small group offers a new possibility of growing into Christ in the company and with the help of others. And it is never simply for its own sake, for the small group also acts as a reminder of the calling to enter every group, every place, every situation, the whole of life with the same attitudes and living by the same practices. As a particular expression of the calling to be a pilgrim people, the small group encapsulates and expresses in miniature the movement and learning of pilgrimage.

Disciples together

Companionship in the pilgrim people of God is the essence of what it means to be a Christian disciple. We are called to the journey of faith in God, and we are blessed to have fellow travellers. These are not simply people going the same way, on a parallel path, each following Jesus. We are given to and for each other to be channels of grace and agents of formation for one another. Even as we are formed and transformed in mission, worship and community, we are set alongside one another needing the gifts and graces, the insights and experience of our sisters and brothers. Sometimes our companions will be in our own home among our families, sometimes wise counsellors, experienced mentors or spiritual friends. Often they will not be identified in any of these categories, but our journeying with them will nevertheless enable us to learn of God and grow to be more Christlike. When there are small groups in the life of the Church, we may choose to join for a variety of reasons or we may decide that at this moment this is not for us. The fact that they appear, designed or seemingly spontaneously, should remind us again of the invitation to companionship and the calling of the Church to be a pilgrim people. It is one way the Church reminds itself that our calling is to be disciples together.

Bibliography

The 1919 Report: The Final and Interim Reports of the Adult Education Committee of the Ministry of Reconstruction 1918–19, Nottingham: Department of Adult Education, University of Nottingham, 1980.

Adams, Edward, 'First Century Models for Paul's Churches: Selected Scholarly Developments since Meeks', in *After the First Urban Christians*, eds Todd D. Still and David G. Horrell, London and New York: Continuum, 2009.

Aelred, *Spiritual Friendship*, ed. Marsha L. Dutton, Collegeville, MN: Liturgical Press, 2010.

Anglican–Methodist Working Party, *Fresh Expressions in the Mission of the Church*, London: Church House Publishing, 2012.

Astley, Jeff, *Ordinary Theology: Looking, Listening and Learning in Theology*, Explorations in Pastoral, Practical and Empirical Theology, Aldershot: Ashgate, 2002.

Atkins, Martyn, *Resourcing Renewal: Shaping Churches for the Emerging Future*, Peterborough: Epworth Press, 2010.

Bandura, A., *Social Learning Theory*, New York: General Learning Press, 1971.

Banks, John, *Group: See How They Run: House Fellowship, the House Church, Class Meetings, the Cell*, London: Epworth Press, 1967.

Banks, Robert, *Paul's Idea of Community: The Early House Churches in their Historical Setting*, Exeter: Paternoster Press, 1980.

Banks, Robert and Julia, *The Church Comes Home*, Peabody, MA: Hendrickson, 1998.

Berger, Peter L., and Thomas Luckmann, *The Social Construction of Reality: A Treatise in the Sociology of Knowledge*, Garden City, NY: Anchor, 1966.

Best, Ernest, *Disciples and Discipleship: Studies in the Gospel According to Mark*, Edinburgh: T. & T. Clark, 1986.

Bunton, Peter, *Cell Groups and House Churches: What History Teaches Us*, Ephrata, PA: House to House Publications, 2001.

Cahn, Peter S., 'Saints with Glasses: Mexican Catholics in Alcoholics Anonymous', *Journal of Contemporary Religion*, 20: 2 (2005).

Cameron, Helen, *Resourcing Mission: Practical Theology for Changing Churches*, London: SCM Press, 2010.

Cameron, Helen, Deborah Bhatti, Catherine Duce, James Sweeney and Clare Watkins, *Talking About God in Practice: Theological Action Research and Practical Theology*, London: SCM Press, 2010.

Cardenal, Ernesto, *The Gospel in Solentiname*, Vol. 2, New York: Orbis Books, 1985.

Cho, Paul Yonggi, *Successful Home Cell Groups*, Plainfield, NJ: Logos International, 1981.

Cotton, Robert, *Reimagining Discipleship: Loving the Local Community*, London: SPCK, 2012.

Croft, Steven J. L., *Transforming Communities: Re-Imagining the Church for the 21st Century*, London: Darton, Longman & Todd, 2002.

Day, Abby, 'Doing Theodicy: An Empirical Study of a Women's Prayer Group', *Journal of Contemporary Religion*, 20: 3 (2005).

Dennis, Marie, Renny Golden and Scott Wright, *Oscar Romero: Reflections on His Life and Writings*, Modern Spiritual Masters Series, Maryknoll, NY: Orbis Books, 2000.

Donahue, B., and Robinson, R., *Building a Church of Small Groups*, Grand Rapids, MI: Zondervan, 2001.

Dougherty Kevin D., 'How Monochrome Is Church Membership? Racial-Ethnic Diversity in Religious Community', *Sociology of Religion*, 64: 1 (2003).

Dougherty, Kevin D., and R. Huyser, 'Racially Diverse Congregations: Organizational Identity and the Accommodation of Difference', *Journal for the Scientific Study of Religion*, 47 (2008)

Dougherty, Kevin D., and Andrew L. Whitehead, 'A Place to Belong: Small Group Involvement in Religious Congregations', *Sociology of Religion*, 72: 1 (2011).

Douglas, Tom, *Survival in Groups*, Buckingham: Open University Press, 1995.

Douglas, Tom, *Survival in Groups: The Basics of Group Membership*, Buckingham and Philadelphia: Open University Press, 1995.

Drane, John, *After McDonaldization*, London: Darton, Longman & Todd, 2008.

Drane, John William, *The McDonaldization of the Church: Spirituality, Creativity, and the Future of the Church*, London: Darton Longman & Todd, 2000.

Dunn, James D. G., *Unity and Diversity in the New Testament: An Inquiry into the Character of Earliest Christianity*, London: SCM Press, 1977.

Dustin, Donna, *The McDonaldization of Social Work*, Aldershot: Ashgate, 2007.

Elliott, Charles, *Praying the Kingdom: Towards a Political Spirituality*, London: Darton, Longman & Todd, 1985.

Emerson, Michael O., and Rodney M. Woo, *People of the Dream: Multi-racial Congregations in the United States*, Princeton: Princeton University Press, 2006.

Francis, Leslie J., David W. Lankshear, and Susan H. Jones, 'The Influence of the Charismatic Movement on Local Church Life: A Comparative Study among Anglican Rural, Urban and Suburban Churches', *Journal of Contemporary Religion*, 15:1 (2000).

Frazee, Randy, *The Connecting Church: Beyond Small Groups to Authentic Community*, Grand Rapids, MI: Zondervan, 2001.

Gehring, Roger W., *House Church and Mission: The Importance of Household Structures in Early Christianity*, Peabody, MA: Hendrickson, 2004.

Gladen, Steve, *Small Groups with Purpose: How to Create Healthy Churches*, Grand Rapids, MI: BakerBooks, 2011.

Gruber, Hans et al., 'Situated Learning and Transfer: Implications for Teaching', in *Learners, Learning and Assessment*, ed. P. Murphy, London: Paul Chapman, 1999.

Guest, Mathew, *Evangelical Identity and Contemporary Culture: A Congregational Study in Innovation*, Studies in Evangelical History and Thought, Milton Keynes: Paternoster, 2007.

Hare, A. Paul, *The Handbook of Small Group Research*, New York: Free Press, 1962.

Harvey, David, 'Cell Church: Its Situation in British Evangelical Culture', *Journal of Contemporary Religion*, 18:1 (2003).

Harvey, David A. ed., *A Contextual and Theological Examination of the British Cell Church Movement* [Electronic Resource], Sheffield: University of Sheffield, 2004.

Hauerwas, Stanley, *Christian Existence Today: Essays on Church, World and Living in Between*, Durham, NC: Labyrinth Press, 1988.

Hauerwas, Stanley, *The Peaceable Kingdom: A Primer in Christian Ethics*, London: SCM Press 2003.

Hay, David, *Something There: The Biology of the Human Spirit*, London: Darton, Longman & Todd, 2006.

Hay, David, and Rebecca Nye, *The Spirit of the Child*, London: Jessica Kingsley, 2006.

Hayes, Dennis, and Robin Wynyard, *The McDonaldization of Higher Education*, Westport, CN: London: Bergin & Garvey, 2002.

Healey, Joseph G., and Jeanne Hinton, *Small Christian Communities Today: Capturing the New Moment*, Maryknoll, NY: Orbis, 2005.

Henderson, D. Michael, *A Model for Making Disciples: John Wesley's Class Meeting*, Nappanee, IN: Evangel Publishing House, 1997.

Hull, John M., *What Prevents Christian Adults from Learning?* London: SCM Press, 1985.

Hunt, Stephen, 'The Alpha Programme: Some Tentative Observations of the State of the Art: Evangelism in the UK', *Journal of Contemporary Religion*, 18: 1 (2003).

Jones, L. Gregory, and Kevin R. Armstrong, *Resurrecting Excellence: Shaping Faithful Christian Ministry*, Grand Rapids, MI: Eerdmans, 2006.

Joyce, Kathleen M., 'The Long Loneliness: Liberal Catholics and the Conservative Church', in *I Come Away Stronger: How Small Groups are Shaping American Religion*, ed. Robert Wuthnow, Grand Rapids, MI: Eerdmans, 1994.

Joyce, Rachel, *The Unlikely Pilgrimage of Harold Fry*, London: Doubleday, 2012.

Kay, William K., *Apostolic Networks in Britain: New Ways of Being Church*, Milton Keynes: Paternoster, 2007.

Kirkpatrick, Thomas G., *Small Groups in the Church: A Handbook for Creating Community*, Bethesda, MD: The Alban Institiute, 1995.

Kraemer, H., *The Theology of the Laity*, London: Lutterworth Press, 1958.

Lave, Jean, and Etienne Wenger, *Situated Learning: Legitimate Peripheral Participation* in Learning in Doing: Social, Cognitive, and Computational Perspectives, Cambridge: Cambridge University Press, 1991.

Levine, John M., and Richard L. Moreland, *Small Groups: Key Readings*, Key Readings in Social Psychology, New York and Hove: Psychology Press, 2006.

Lloyd-Jones, David Martyn, *The Puritans: Their Origins and Successors*, London: Banner of Truth Trust, 1987.

Martin, Nancy J., 'Small Groups in Big Churches', PhD thesis, University of Arizona, 2007.

McGuire, Meredith B., *Pentecostal Catholics: Power, Charisma, and Order in a Religious Movement*, Philadelphia, PA: Temple University Press, 1982.

Meeks, Wayne A., *The First Urban Christians: The Social World of the Apostle Paul*, 2nd edn, New Haven and London: Yale University Press, 2003.

Meggitt, Justin J., *Paul, Poverty and Survival: Studies of the New Testament and Its World*, Edinburgh: T. & T. Clark, 1998.

Methodist Church, *Called to Love and Praise*, London: TMPC, 1999.

Methodist Church, *Time to Talk of God*, London: TMPC, 2005.

Mills, Theodore M., *The Sociology of Small Groups*, 2nd edn, Prentice-Hall Foundations of Modern Sociology Series, Englewood Cliffs and London: Prentice-Hall, 1984.

Minear, Paul S., *Matthew: The Teacher's Gospel*, Eugene, OR: Wipf & Stock, 1982.

Moltmann, Jürgen, *The Open Church: Invitation to a Messianic Life-Style*, London: SCM Press, 1978.

Moon, Jennifer A., *Reflection in Learning and Professional Development: Theory and Practice*, Abingdon and New York: Routledge, 2000.

Neighbour, Ralph W., *Where Do We Go from Here? A Guidebook for the Cell Group Churches*, Houston, TX: Touch Publications, 1990.

Nichols, Bridget, 'A Tune Beyond Us, Yet Ourselves: Ordinary Worship and Ordinary Theology', in *Exploring Ordinary Theology: Everyday Christian Believing and the Church*, eds Jeff Astley and Leslie J. Francis, Farnham and Burlington, VT: Ashgate, 2013.

Oakes, Peter, *Reading Romans in Pompeii: Paul's Letter at Ground Level*, London: SPCK, 2009.

Olson, Daniel V. A., 'Making Disciples in a Liberal Protestant Church', in *I Come Away Stronger: How Small Groups are Shaping American Religion*, ed. Robert Wuthnow, Grand Rapids, MI: Eerdmans, 1994.

Ortiz, Juan Carlos, and Jamie Buckingham, *Call to Discipleship*, Plainfield, NJ: Logos International, 1975.

Osiek, Carolyn, and David L. Balch, *Families in the New Testament World: Households and House Churches*, Family, Religion, and Culture, Louisville, KY: Westminster John Knox Press, 1997.

Phillips, Peter, *National Biblical Literacy Survey 2008*, Durham: CODEC, St John's College, University of Durham, 2009.

Potter, Phil, *The Challenge of Cell Church: Getting to Grips with Cell Church Values*, Oxford: Bible Reading Fellowship, 2001.

Pratt, J. H., 'The Principles of Class Treatment and Their Application to Various Chronic Diseases', *Hospital Social Services* 6:6 (1922)

Prior, David, *The Church in the Home*, Basingstoke: Marshall Pickering, 1983.

Putnam, Jim, *Real-Life Discipleship: Building Churches that Make Disciples*, Colorado Springs, CO: NavPress, 2010.

Putnam, R. T., and Hilda Borko, 'What Do New Views of Knowledge and Thinking Have to Say About Research on Teacher Learning?' *Educational Researcher*, 29: 1 (2000).

Ritzer, G., *The McDonaldization of Society*, Thousand Oaks, London and New Delhi: Pine Forge Press, 1996.

Robinson, John A. T., *Essays on Being the Church in the World*, London: SCM Press, 1960.

Rogers, Carl R., *Encounter Groups*, Harmondsworth: Penguin, 1985, (1970).

Savage, Helen, 'Ordinary Learning', in *Exploring Ordinary Theology: Everyday Christian Believing and the Church*, eds Jeff Astley and Leslie J. Francis, Farnham and Burlington, VT: Ashgate, 2013.

Scandrette, Mark, *Practicing the Way of Jesus: Life Together in the Kingdom of Love*, Downers Grove, IL: InterVarsity Press, 2011.

Sheppard, David, *Bias to the Poor*, London: Hodder & Stoughton, 1983.

Skinner, M., *House Groups*, London: Epworth Press, 1969.

Smart, Barry, *Resisting McDonaldization*, London: SAGE, 1999.

Smith, James K. A., *Desiring the Kingdom: Worship, Worldview and Cultural Formation*, Grand Rapids, MI: Baker Academic, 2009.

Trudinger, Ron, *Cells for Life: Home Groups – God's Strategy for Church Growth*, Eastbourne: Kingsway, 1983.

Veling, Terry A., *Practical Theology: On Earth as It Is in Heaven*, Maryknoll, NY: Orbis Books, 2005.

Vickers, John, *A Dictionary of Methodism in Britain and Ireland*, Peterborough: Epworth Press, 2000.

Wagner, Peter C., 'Third Wave', in *International Dictionary of Pentecostal and Charismatic Movements*, ed. S. M. Burgess, Grand Rapids, MI: Zondervan, 2002.

Walker, Andrew, *Restoring the Kingdom: The Radical Christianity of the House Church Movement*, London: Hodder & Stoughton, 1985.

Walton, Roger L., 'Disciples Together: The Small Group as a Vehicle for Discipleship Formation', *Journal of Adult Theological Education* 8:2 (2012).

Walton, Roger L., 'Ordinary Discipleship', in *Exploring Ordinary Theology: Everyday Christian Believing and the Church*, eds Jeff Astley and Leslie J. Francis, Farnham and Burlington, VT: Ashgate, 2013.

Walton, Roger L., *The Reflective Disciple: Learning to Live as Faithful Followers of Jesus in the Twenty-first Century*, London: SCM Press, 2010.

Walton, Roger L., 'The Teaching and Learning of Theological Reflection: Case Studies of Practice', PhD thesis University of Durham, 2002.

Watling, Tony, 'Experiencing Alpha: Finding and Embodying the Spirit and Being Transformed – Empowerment and Control in a (Charismatic) Worldview', *Journal of Contemporary Religion*, 20:1, (2005).

Watson, David L., *Covenant Discipleship: Christian Formation Through Mutual Accountability,* Eugene, OR: Wipf & Stock, 2002.

West, Liz, and Trevor Withers, *Walking Together: Making 21st Century Disciples*, Harpenden: Cell UK Ministries, 2011.

Wingate, Andrew, *Does Theological Education Make a Difference? Global Lessons in Mission and Ministry from India and Britain*, Geneva: WCC Publications, 1999.

Wright, Tom, *The Lord and His Prayer*, London: SPCK, 1996.

Wuthnow, Robert, *Sharing the Journey: Support Groups and America's New Quest for Community*, New York and London: Free Press, 1996.